For discussion questions on each chapter,
visit the title description page for *Sightings of the Savior* at
<www.ivpress.com>.
The direct link is
<www.gospelcom.net/cgi-ivpress/book.pl/code=3232>.

SIGHTINGS
of the
SAVIOR

Meeting Jesus When We Need Him Most

—♦♦♦—

RICK EZELL

IVP

InterVarsity Press
Downers Grove, Illinois

InterVarsity Press
P.O. Box 1400, Downers Grove, IL 60515-1426
World Wide Web: www.ivpress.com
E-mail: mail@ivpress.com

InterVarsity Press® is the book-publishing division of InterVarsity Christian Fellowship/USA®, a student
movement active on campus at hundreds of universities, colleges and schools of nursing in the United States of
America, and a member movement of the International Fellowship of Evangelical Students. For information
about local and regional activities, write Public Relations Dept., InterVarsity Christian Fellowship/USA, 6400
Schroeder Rd., P.O. Box 7895, Madison, WI 53707-7895, or visit the IVCF website at <www.ivcf.org>.

All Scripture quotations, unless otherwise indicated, are taken from the Holy Bible, New International
Version®. NIV®. Copyright ©1973, 1978, 1984 by International Bible Society. Used by permission of
Zondervan Publishing House. All rights reserved.

Cover and interior design: Cindy Kiple
Cover image (leaf): Ryan McVay/Getty Images
Cover image (The Shipwreck, 1873): Christie's Images/Bridgeman Art Library
Interior images: Gettyone
ISBN 0-8308-3232-7

Printed in the United States of America ∞

Library of Congress Cataloging-in-Publication Data

Ezell, Rick, 1956-
    Sightings of the Savior: meeting Jesus when we need Him most/Rick
Ezell.
        p. cm.
    ISBN 0-83-8-3232-7 (pbk.: alk. paper)
    1. Christian life—Baptist authors. I. Title.
    BV4501.3.E95 2003
    232—dc21
                                                                            2003006748

P	17	16	15	14	13	12	11	10	9	8	7	6	5	4	3	2	1
Y	17	16	15	14	13	12	11	10	09	08	07	06	05	04	03		

CONTENTS

—⁓—

1

BUT THEN YOU CAME

Jesus Crosses Our Path

*I*n those days Caesar Augustus issued a decree that a census should be taken of the entire Roman world. (This was the first census that took place while Quirinius was governor of Syria.) And everyone went to his own town to register.

So Joseph also went up from the town of Nazareth in Galilee to Judea, to Bethlehem the town of David, because he belonged to the house and line of David. He went there to register with Mary, who was pledged to be married to him and was expecting a child. While they were there, the time came for the baby to be born, and she gave birth to her firstborn, a son. She wrapped him in cloths and placed him in a manger, because there was no room for them in the inn.

And there were shepherds living out in the fields nearby, keeping watch over their flocks at night. An angel of the Lord appeared to them, and the glory of the Lord shone around them, and they were terrified. But the angel said to them, "Do not be afraid. I bring you good news of great joy that will be for all the people. Today in the town of David a Savior has been born to you; he is Christ the Lord. This will be a sign to you: You will find a baby wrapped in cloths and lying in a manger."

LUKE 2:1-12

$\mathcal{S}$he was fifteen and he was seventeen when they met. All through high school they dated, and after high school it was not a surprise to anyone that they married. Four years later she was standing in her kitchen with a pile of dirty dishes in the sink, two children at her feet, and a pile of dirty diapers in the corner. Tears were streaming down her face. Looking back, she could never be quite sure why she made the decision, but she did. She took off her apron and walked out.

She called that night and her young husband answered the phone. He was, understandably, quite worried and also quite angry. "Where are you?" he said, his concern and his anger fighting for control of his voice.

"How are the children?" she asked, ignoring his question.

"Well, if you mean have they been fed, they have. I've also put them to bed. They are wondering, just as I am, where you are? What are you doing?"

She hung up the phone that night, but it wasn't the last of the phone calls. She called almost every week for the next three months. Her husband, knowing that something was seriously wrong, began to plead with her to come home. He would tell her that the children were with their grandparents during the day and were well cared for. He would tell her that he loved her. He would tell her how much they all missed her, and then he would try to find out where she was. Whenever the conversation turned to her whereabouts, she would hang up.

Finally, the young husband could stand it no longer. He took their savings and hired a private detective to find his wife. The detective reported that the runaway wife was in a third-rate hotel in Des Moines, Iowa. The young man borrowed money from his in-laws, bought a plane ticket and flew to Des Moines. After taking a cab to the hotel, he climbed the stairs to his wife's room on the third floor. With doubt in his eyes and perspiration on his forehead, his trembling hand knocked on the door. When his wife opened the door, he forgot his prepared speech and said, "We love you so much. Won't you come home?" She fell apart in his arms. They went home together.

One evening, some weeks later, the children were in bed and he and his wife were sitting in the living room before the fire. He finally got up enough courage to ask the question that had haunted him for so many months. He asked, "Why wouldn't you come home? Why, when I told you over and over again that I loved you and missed you, didn't you come home?"

"Because," she said with profound simplicity, "before those were only words. *But then you came.*"

WHEN GOD CAME TO US

On the first Christmas over two thousand years ago, God *came* to earth to live among us. The human mind is boggled by that fact. No flaming chariots brought God into the world, and no royal entourage greeted him. God entered the world as a helpless baby in a stable with a trough for a bed.

The stable stank of urine, dung and animals. The dirt floor was hard, the hay was scarce, and cobwebs clung to the ceiling. Off to one side sat a group of shepherds, perhaps perplexed, perhaps in awe, but no doubt in amazement. Near the young mother sat the weary father. Now that the excitement had subsided a bit, now that Mary and the baby were comfortable, he leaned against the wall of the stable, overcome with weariness. Mary was wide awake. She looked into the face of the baby. Her son.

The baby Jesus looked like anything but God. His face was wrinkled and red. His cry, though strong and healthy, was still the helpless and piercing cry of a baby. He was absolutely dependent on Mary for his survival.

God came into the world in a backwoods village through the womb of a teenager and in the presence of a carpenter. In one magnificent moment God moved beyond words and came to us.

GOD IS HERE

The last place I expected graffiti was on a restroom stall door of my church. Serving as a minister to a growing, suburban congregation afforded little time to oneself. Consequently, I would often withdraw to a restroom at the opposite end of the building. There I was free of most interruptions and distractions.

In small but clear letters etched in the brown door at eye level were three words: *God was here.* An innocent gag, probably written by one of the creative teenagers I worked with. Admittedly, reading such a statement in a bathroom does make one slightly uncomfortable.

A week later I returned to my place of quiet. I needed peace from the frustrations of a crowded day. I noticed that the graffiti had been changed, and better yet, it was more theologically accurate. Someone had crossed out *was* and written above it *is.* In a quiet restroom the message of hope was proclaimed: *God is here.*

When Jesus came, he was the message that the angels announced, the shepherds heard, the wise men sought, Herod feared and the world did not even notice. It was the message that Mary held and that Joseph admired. It was the message wrapped in cloths. It was the little baby Jesus. The man was the message. And his message would intersect the lives of everyone he came into contact with: God is here, crossing our paths.

Jesus, God's one and only Son, became a man. He was God in a suit of flesh. He was the visible expression of the invisible deity. God was speaking in a language that we could understand. God was identifying with the frailties and tragedies of the human race. God was announcing to the world: "I'm here!"

God came to us. The omnipotent, in one instant, made himself breakable. He who is spirit became human flesh and blood. He who is larger than the universe became a tiny embryo. And he who sustains the world with a word chose to be dependent upon the nourishment of a young girl.

The apostle John uses one word to embody this revelation of God: *dwelt*. "The Word became flesh, and *dwelt* among us" (John 1:14 NASB). Eugene Petersen in The Message paraphrases this verse, "The Word became flesh and blood, and moved into the neighborhood" (John 1:14 The Message). *Dwelt* literally means "to live in a tent." Military folk would understand "to bivouac." Theologians might say "to tabernacle." In the Old Testament *dwelt* and its derivatives literally denote residence. Often the word was used to depict the glorious presence of God that resided in the tabernacle and Solomon's temple. When Jesus became flesh and blood, he moved into the neighborhood, took up residence and tabernacled among us.

Before Jesus was born, God visited his people, performing mighty and miraculous works. God's people would stack stones or erect a synagogue in honor of God's revelation. The physical erection of monuments and buildings was their way of saying, "God was here." The power and presence of God had visited them in a place; in order not to forget, they constructed a reminder. But when Jesus entered the world the verb tense changed from past to present—from *was* to *is*. God is present in all of his splendor and glory. We don't have to erect structures to remind us of God's visited presence. God is already here.

WHAT DOES IT ALL MEAN?

God came among us. It is as though we were looking at God through one of those snowy, glass-covered balls and couldn't clearly see God, so Jesus stepped out of the encasement and took up residence on this planet so we could better understand him and know him.

Jesus came from God. This is important. Jesus was not some self-appointed religious leader seeking to make a buck off of helpless and hopeless people. He was God's Son, his emissary, his flesh and blood coming to this sin-stained planet on behalf of the Father.

Some years ago I regularly visited a woman in a nursing home. Nursing homes have improved greatly in recent years, but this one had a foul stench and the help was less than cordial. In this environment a dear saint lived. Clara Bell had once been a brilliant teacher; even at eighty-seven she retained more wit than most of us will ever have. Our visits were genuine and stimulating. As her pastor, I was one of her few contacts with the outside world. Of course there were a few church people who visited, but most of her family lived far away and rarely visited. One day I asked her, "Why do you always want to see me?"

"Because you come for God."

This answer helped me understand the function of all Christ-followers in a new and profound way. Maybe she liked me as a person, but primarily I was a representative of God in a way no one else could be.

In like manner, when Jesus visited this planet there was a stench from the sin that pervaded the place. People's souls were left uncared for. And then Jesus came. He came as God's representative bearing both his love and authority.

Jesus came to show us God. The apostle John wrote, "The Word became flesh and made his dwelling among us. We have seen his glory, the glory of the One and Only, who came from the Father, full of grace and truth" (John 1:14). W. E. Vine writes that the word *truth* literally means "that which is open to view, that which is unconcealed, that which is transparent." In Moffat's translation of the Bible, this word is translated as "reality." Jesus was full of grace and reality. Jesus was real—the most real person who has ever lived. When Jesus came he was really man and really God.

When Jesus became a man he showed that God was not merely a principle but a person; not a myth, but a man who was God at the same time; not a figment of someone's imagination, but a living presence. Jesus was not an idea of God, but God himself in human form.

Two young men on a battlefield in World War II made it to the safety of a foxhole in the midst of enemy fire. As they looked out before them across the battlefield they perceived the horror of dead and dying men. Twisted barbed wire, the earth scarred with deep holes left by cannon fire. Some men lay lifeless, others cried out for help. Finally one of the men yelled, "Where in the hell is God?" As they continued to watch and to listen, soon they noticed two medics, identified by the red cross on their arms and their helmets, carefully making their way across the perilous scene. As they watched, the medics stopped and began to load a wounded soldier onto their stretcher. Once loaded they began to work their way to safety. As the scene unfolded before them, the other soldier now boldly answered the honest but piercing question of his friend: "There is God! There is God!"

When Jesus came, it was his way of saying: "Here is God! Here is God!" He came in the midst of the loneliness and the horror of a world gone mad. In the chaos and confusion, Jesus announced that God is here. Christ has come among us to show us who and what God is in a way that renews us, gives us hope, and demonstrates compassion.

Jesus came to demonstrate God's love. When Jesus came he didn't just talk about love. He loved. He didn't just preach on forgiveness. He forgave. He didn't just proclaim the necessity of justice and righteousness. He attacked the unrighteous institutions of his day. He became flesh.

His love is so incredible and so wonderful that it almost defies understanding. Love, if it really is love, expresses itself. God knew that he would have to personify his love before we could understand it.

It is nice to think that God loved the world. But when Jesus came God's love was no longer words, platitudes or clichés. "For God so loved the world that he gave his one and only Son" (John 3:16). Jesus Christ, the embodiment of love, came to us. Jesus loved us so much that the comforts of heaven could not distract him, the walls of glory could not encase him, the voices of the angels could not dissuade him, and the power of deity could not hold him. He had to come; he could do nothing else. He stepped out of his heavenly home to take his place in a dirty, smelly world.

Jesus came to remind us that we were are not abandoned. I heard Steve Brown on the radio telling about the ugliest car he had ever seen. It had a large gash on its side; the door was held together with bailing wire; many places on the car were rusted out. The muffler was loose and, with every bump, was hitting the street sending sparks in every direction. It was hard to tell the original color of the car. The rust had eaten away much of the original paint, and so much of the car had been painted over with so many different colors that any one of them, or none of them, could have been the first coat. The most interesting thing about the car was the bumper sticker. It read, "This is not an abandoned car."

We live in a fallen world. It is ugly and depressing. Everywhere we turn we find tragedy and heartache. We are sitting on the verge of disaster. Sometimes the effort to keep on keeping on doesn't seem worth it. Guilt, loneliness, hurt and fear become constant companions. One wonders if anyone, especially God, cares. But a long time ago, in a manger, a baby was born. It was a sign. It read, "This is not an abandoned world."

When Jesus came, God gave us the assurance that he had not

abandoned us. What the angel said to the shepherds was the same thing God is saying to us today, "Do not be afraid. I bring you good news of great joy that will be for all the people. Today in the town of David a Savior has been born to you; he is Christ the Lord" (Luke 2:10-11).

Even though we may not understand all that is happening to us and to our world, we are in good hands. God is not in a panic; he is still in control of our world. While circumstances may indicate panic at every turn, God came to say that he can understand the complexities of humanity and will touch people where they hurt the most.

CROSSING THE PATH OF JESUS

In the pages that follow are the stories of men and women, not much different from you and me, who crossed the path of Jesus. Some of these unsuspecting people were outcasts while others were the religious and political elite; some were living in squalor while others were surrounded by luxury. In each case, Jesus offered his comfort and help, and each person walked away from an encounter with Jesus changed. As demonstrated throughout all of Jesus' time on this earth, and even today, he meets people at their point of need. Jesus wants to intersect our lives where we hurt in order to bring his soothing balm of grace.

~2~

THE HARDEST THING
TO DO

Jesus Meets Our Needs

*O*n *the eighth day, when it was time to circumcise him, he was named Jesus, the name the angel had given him before he had been conceived.*

When the time of their purification according to the Law of Moses had been completed, Joseph and Mary took him to Jerusalem to present him to the Lord (as it is written in the Law of the Lord, "Every firstborn male is to be consecrated to the

Lord"), and to offer a sacrifice in keeping with what is said in the Law of the Lord: "a pair of doves or two young pigeons."

Now there was a man in Jerusalem called Simeon, who was righteous and devout. He was waiting for the consolation of Israel, and the Holy Spirit was upon him. It had been revealed to him by the Holy Spirit that he would not die before he had seen the Lord's Christ. Moved by the Spirit, he went into the temple courts. When the parents brought in the child Jesus to do for him what the custom of the Law required, Simeon took him in his arms and praised God, saying:

"Sovereign Lord, as you have promised,
    you now dismiss your servant in peace.
For my eyes have seen your salvation,
    which you have prepared in the sight of all people,
a light for revelation to the Gentiles
    and for glory to your people Israel."

The child's father and mother marveled at what was said about him. Then Simeon blessed them and said to Mary, his mother: "This child is destined to cause the falling and rising of many in Israel, and to be a sign that will be spoken against, so that the thoughts of many hearts will be revealed. And a sword will pierce your own soul too." . . .

When Joseph and Mary had done everything required by the
Law of the Lord, they returned to Galilee to their own town
of Nazareth. And the child grew and became strong; he was
filled with wisdom, and the grace of God was upon him.

LUKE 2:21-40

*Y*ears ago in Great Britain, a family had a dream of traveling
to the United States. The Clarks had worked and saved every
precious dollar so their entire family, including nine children,
could cross the Atlantic to live in America. It took years. Finally
enough money had been saved. Passports were obtained. Res-
ervations on a new ocean liner were made. Tickets were purchased.

The entire family was filled with anticipation and excitement about their new life in a new country. Seven days before
their scheduled departure, a dog bit the youngest son. The doctor bandaged his wound, gave him medication, but hung a yel-
low sheet on the Clarks' front door. Because of the possibility
of rabies, the entire family was quarantined for fourteen days.

The family's dream was dashed. They would not make the trip to America as they had planned. The father, filled with disappointment and anger, stomped to the dock to watch the ship leave—without his family aboard. The father shed tears of disappointment and cursed both his son and God for their misfortune.

Five days later, the tragic news spread throughout England. The *Titanic* had sunk. Waiting sometimes turns out to be a blessing.

WAITING—THE HARDEST THING

Because of a set of unfortunate circumstances, my wife and I were living in a place and serving in a ministry that was not our long-term choice. I sought other positions. One opportunity availed itself. They made an offer, but it didn't seem right. So we turned it down, knowing that something more to our liking would present itself soon. It did not.

We continued to serve and to wait for well over a year before another offer was made. This was a most difficult time. We doubted our decision regarding the previous opportunity. We questioned God. We wondered when he would show up and do something about our situation. Our faith was stretched and pulled. Was God trying to show us something?

Was God trying to reveal himself?

Many times, I don't like to wait. In some circumstances, I am not a patient person. Often, I am like a child at Christmas, eagerly anticipating the time to open presents. Each hour seems like an eternity. When the time arrives, I can't move fast enough to the Christmas tree so the presents can be opened.

Waiting may be the hardest single thing we have to do. In the Bible, waiting is closely associated with faith. Sometimes the words are used interchangeably. While we may not like it, waiting is a necessary part of the Christian life. What God does in us while we wait is as important as what we are waiting for. Waiting is not easy. It may bring pain. It will try us and test us. It demands patience. It exacts a price.

The promise of the Old Testament was that a Messiah would come. But Israel had to wait—generation after generation, century after century. And when the Messiah came, only those who were watching recognized his coming. For one man in particular, his waiting turned out to be his greatest blessing.

ONE MAN WHO WAITED

The man who recognized the Savior, who paid the enormous toll of waiting, was Simeon. For years Simeon looked for the Messiah. God had assured Simeon that before his death he would see the Christ. Simeon had lived holding on to God's promise to bring redemption to his people. That one hope, that one vision, that one dream, had been the center of his life.

And now on a day that was not unlike any of the hundreds of other days in Jerusalem, all of his hopes and fears were about to be met.

Mary and Joseph traveled the five short miles from Bethlehem to Jerusalem to present Jesus in the temple, according to the Jewish law. Hebrew parents came several times to fulfill the requirements of the law at the birth of a first son. First, eight days after his birth, Jesus was circumcised—the mark of the covenant and the time at which the male received his name, his identity. This rite was so sacred, so important in Jewish tradition that Jews would circumcise the male on the eighth day, even if the eighth day fell on the Sabbath. Second, thirty-one days after his birth, Jesus was presented to the Lord. This ritual was called the "Redemption of the First Born." It recognized that the first fruits of all creation were God's and should be sacrificed to God. The covenant made possible the sacrifice of animals in place of children. In Jewish tradition the first-born male belonged to God. Parents gave an offering to the temple priest to symbolically purchase their child back into their family. The third ritual was the "Purification of the Mother" that occurred on the fortieth day after a son's birth. (For daughters this ritual occurred on the eightieth day.) Often a lamb was sacrificed; but if the parents were poor, the offering was a pair of doves or two young pigeons, as was Mary and Joseph's offering.

In the temple courts, Mary and Joseph fulfilled the ancient traditions. On one of their trips, a man named Simeon, who was old as the hills, with large, rheumy eyes and spittle in his beard, shuffled about, because in his heart, God had told him that he "would not die before he had seen the Lord's Christ" (Luke 2:26).

All these years he had waited for the Messiah to come. His dream was that someday he would meet the One whom God sent to be the Savior of the world. The people of Israel had waited hundreds of years for the Messiah to come. Simeon waited. He longed. He yearned.

So here he was in the temple courts frightening all the mothers who were bringing their babies to the priests. Every time he saw a blue blanket he ran over. "Yeah, it's a boy, it's a boy. Let me see." He came to Mary and said, "Let me hold him." She was scared. He was old and feeble. Simeon saw the baby of Mary and Joseph and knew this was no ordinary infant.

How did he know? Did the baby have a halo over his head? Did he emit some sweet-smelling fragrance? Did he have light beaming from his face? How did Simeon know?

Mary's anxiety over a feeble man holding her baby was nothing compared to the fear that was created by what Simeon said next. "This child is destined to cause the falling and rising of many in Israel, and to be a sign that will be spoken against, so that the thoughts of many hearts will be revealed. And a sword will pierce your own soul too" (Luke 2:34-35). Simeon revealed to Mary that Jesus' reign as Savior and King on this earth would not include a hero's welcome, or a ticker-tape parade or a life of comfort and ease. Jesus would not be a political savior to rescue Israel from Roman occupation. Jesus would be controversial. Some would love him; others would hate him. He would suffer. So, too, would Mary and Joseph. Simeon's words pointed to the crucifixion, Jesus dying on the cross, where his mother would watch the suffering Messiah.

Simeon, why did you have to go and spoil everything like that? It was a nice service. The priest was in rare form. No babies wailed, none threw up on the attendants, and you ruined it. Why? Simeon knew that this child had come into the world to die for the sins of humankind. Simeon knew that the baby Jesus was the Savior of the world.

Simeon crossed the path of the Savior. Now his life was complete. He was ready to die. His hope had materialized. His dream became reality. And it was worth the wait. He saw Jesus, the Messiah. He held him in his arms. He wanted nothing more. Joy had filled his heart. Simeon knew that when the Messiah crossed his path, it was the ultimate experience of life. Nothing in the world would come close to matching it. Jesus was worth the wait.

WHILE YOU WAIT, REMEMBER

Simeon's story is not unlike our stories. We, too, long to see the Savior. We, too, have a dream of meeting God incarnate. We, too, often wait. These times are not easy times, but in the end we can say with Simeon, "It was worth the wait." Waiting, indeed, can turn out to be our greatest blessing.

What does Simeon's story teach us?

Our search for Jesus can't wait. Simeon spent his entire life committed to the task of looking for the Messiah. His look was not a casual observance. He did not think nonchalantly, "I'll see him if he jumps out in front of me." His search was intentional. It was an honest, sincere search for the Savior. He would wait for the Savior to show up, but he could not wait to begin the search.

Shortly before his death, ex-Beatle George Harrison was asked about his spiritual journey. The question was appropriate, since it was Harrison who introduced the Beatles to Eastern religion in the 1960s and (after the group broke up) wrote the song

"My Sweet Lord" (a hymn of praise to the Hindu deity Krishna). Until the end of his life, Harrison continued to investigate spiritual matters. He summed up his priorities this way: "Everything else in life can wait, but the search for God cannot wait."

Simeon would agree with that assessment, and so should we. If we don't find God, we have missed the very reason for our existence. Compared to knowing the One who made us, everything else is just crumbs.

Deep inside, all people have this hunger. God's handprint is on us. His very breath spoke the world into existence. He set eternity in our hearts. We, therefore, are incurably spiritual by nature. That's why every human society—no matter how primitive—has some concept of a higher power, some vision of a reality that goes beyond the natural. On one level, this explains why science has not eradicated religion from the earth. Technological achievement cannot meet the deepest needs of the human heart. That's why millions of people read their horoscopes every morning, and millions more call psychic hotlines.

People are hungry for spiritual truth and if they cannot find it by normal means, they will reach for anyone or anything that claims to give them an answer. Something in us drives us to seek ultimate meaning outside ourselves. God puts that *something* inside us. Augustine gave us the oft-quoted prayer, "You have made us for yourself, and our hearts are restless until they find their rest in you." All of us are on a search for the Savior. We desperately want to find him.

The search for God can't wait. No one lives forever, not even ex-Beatles. Searching for God is good; finding him is much better. Simeon found Jesus. I suspect that the reason you are reading this book is that you want to find him too. But it's imperative that we know where to search.

We will find Jesus if we look for him in the right place. Sometimes we don't find Jesus because we aren't looking for him in the right place.

A South African discovered one of the world's largest diamonds. It was the size of a small lemon. He wanted to get it to the London office as safely and as quickly as possible. He found a steel box and hired four men to carry the box to London by hand. When it arrived, the steel box was unlocked. Much to their surprise a diamond wasn't in there, just a black lump of coal. They were shocked. They didn't know what to do. Three days later, by parcel post in an ordinary box, the diamond arrived in the London office. The South African thought that no one would pay any attention to an ordinary box.

Two thousand years ago, God came wrapped in an ordinary

body in a way no one expected, in a place that was as remote and off the beaten path as one could imagine. Who would ever look for God there?

Simeon did. He looked for Jesus and found him in the most ordinary place. Others had looked for the Savior in the spectacular. Others thought the Messiah would come in great military might. Still others longed for the Christ in a cosmopolitan city. And all the while Jesus was being born as an ordinary baby to humble, peasant parents, in a tiny village in a remote back alley of the world. His parents presented him in the temple in the traditional, ancient ways, with no fanfare. And on this day the only one who found him was a man who happened to be looking for the Savior in the right place at the right time.

Simeon knew that the Messiah would be born of Jewish parents who would follow Jewish law. He trusted that these parents would come to the temple to fulfill the required rituals. He knew his best chance for finding the Savior was in the temple, so he went there each day.

And where is the best place to find Jesus these days? Jesus can be found in almost any place today, but for me the best location is God's house—the church. It's true I can find God in music, in the arts, in nature. But my best chance of finding Jesus is in church. I'm going to follow Simeon's lead and look for the

Savior in church surrounded by God's people, singing songs of praise to God, listening to God's spokesman deliver a message from God's Word.

Wherever you are, finding Jesus requires faith. We can learn a lot about finding Jesus from Simeon. Who was Simeon? He was a righteous and devout man. What was he waiting for? "The consolation of Israel," the Messiah, the Savior. Where was Simeon? He was waiting in the courts of the temple. Why was he there? The Spirit had moved him. Here was a man with the right heart, in his right mind, in the right place, with the right focus and the right faith. No wonder he saw the Savior.

Simeon must have wondered if God was true to his word. He must have thought a time or two, "God, I'm running out of years here. I can't live forever. If you are going to send the Messiah, don't you think you had better do it pretty soon?" And God must have reminded him time and time again: "Your job is to trust, to wait, to accept my timing. That is all. You keep your heart right; I'll keep my promise."

Two different people can have the same desire to find God and be in the same worship service. One walks away saying, "That was boring," while the other walks away saying, "I felt God's touch. I sensed his presence. I heard him speak to me." The difference, among other things, is their faith.

The story of Simeon teaches us that God proves himself faithful. Because I waited, God provided an opportunity and a church asked me to come to be its pastor. It's the church I've served for the last fifteen years. His timing is perfect. Our part is to trust with a confident, disciplined, patient waiting for the appearing of the Savior. God seeks to reveal himself to us. He wants to cross our paths. And he will.

When we focus on the Savior in confident trust, we too will see him. And when we do, we will realize, like Simeon, that waiting can actually turn out to be our greatest blessing.

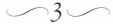

3

WHEN WE JUST DON'T GET IT

Jesus Challenges Our Traditions

*T*hen some Pharisees and teachers of the law came to Jesus from Jerusalem and asked, "Why do your disciples break the tradition of the elders? They don't wash their hands before they eat!"

Jesus replied, "And why do you break the command of God for the sake of your tradition? For God said, 'Honor your father and mother' and 'Anyone who curses his father or mother must be put to death.' But you say that if a man says to his fa-

ther or mother, 'Whatever help you might otherwise have received from me is a gift devoted to God,' he is not to 'honor his
father' with it. Thus you nullify the word of God for the sake
of your tradition. You hypocrites! Isaiah was right when he
prophesied about you:

" 'These people honor me with their lips,

   but their hearts are far from me.

They worship me in vain;

   their teachings are but rules taught by men.' "

Jesus called the crowd to him and said, "Listen and understand. What goes into a man's mouth does not make him 'unclean,' but what comes out of his mouth, that is what makes
him 'unclean.' "

Then the disciples came to him and asked, "Do you know that
the Pharisees were offended when they heard this?"

He replied, "Every plant that my heavenly Father has not
planted will be pulled up by the roots. Leave them; they are
blind guides. If a blind man leads a blind man, both will fall
into a pit."

Peter said, "Explain the parable to us."

"Are you still so dull?" Jesus asked them. "Don't you see that

whatever enters the mouth goes into the stomach and then out
of the body? But the things that come out of the mouth come
from the heart, and these make a man 'unclean.' For out of the
heart come evil thoughts, murder, adultery, sexual immor-
ality, theft, false testimony, slander. These are what make a
man 'unclean'; but eating with unwashed hands does not make
him 'unclean.' "

MATTHEW 15:1-20

*T*he Pharisees were Jesus' biggest nemeses. They were the religious elite of Jesus' day. They knew the law. In fact, they added
laws to the original ten as a sort of fence to protect people from
violating the commandments, either through oversight or accident. They kept track of every jot and tittle. They always seemed
to be in the crowd where Jesus was, watching from a distance.
They sought to expose him if he made a mistake.

On one occasion, Jesus and his disciples were in Gennesaret,
near the Sea of Galilee. People were being healed, souls were

being saved, and then the Pharisees showed up unannounced. Notice two additional words that Matthew included in the text: "Then some Pharisees and teachers of the law came to Jesus *from Jerusalem*" (Matthew 15:1, emphasis added). Intentionally they journeyed seventy-five miles from Jerusalem to Gennesaret to question and test Jesus. (Due to the difficulties of travel, seventy-five miles then would be like 750 miles now.)

On this occasion the Pharisees moved from observing Jesus to questioning him. The encounter between Jesus and the Pharisees was more than a meeting between religious figures. It was a collision between two opposing views of salvation.

The Pharisees thought salvation was purchased; Jesus offered it as a gift. They thought man's job was to earn it; Jesus said man's job was to accept it. The Pharisees were legalists bound by tradition, and they executed their judgment on anyone who differed from their opinion.

On this day they came to Jesus and asked why the disciples ate with unwashed hands. It was not a question about personal hygiene, but about ceremonial purification. The book of Leviticus prescribed ceremonial washings. The Pharisees had supplemented the law with their traditions regarding the occasions, the amount of water, the number of rinses and the use of one or both hands. In other words, they had translated personal beliefs into prescribed behavior.

Jesus, in typical rabbinical style, answered their question with a question. Jesus asked the Pharisees about their practice known as *corban*. *Corban* referred to something that was devoted to God as a gift. The Pharisees used it as a loophole to excuse themselves from assisting their aging parents. Here's how it worked: the Pharisees would designate their monetary gifts to the temple to be used for the care of their elderly parents. But the money would not get to the caretakers of their parents. It was misappropriated back into the Pharisees' pockets. It became a money-laundering scheme.

Their laws regarding the ceremonial washing of hands had violated the Word of God. Their practice of *corban* had nullified the laws of Moses. The Pharisees' actions, and everyone's knowledge of what they were doing with money intended for their parents, had deprived the laws of legal force.

Jesus lost his temper and called them hypocrites and frauds. He quoted from Isaiah: "These people honor me with their lips, but their hearts are far from me. They worship me in vain; their teachings are but rules taught by men" (Matthew 15:8-9). The Pharisees had substituted the teachings of men for the truth of God. They were using their religion to appear religious because they believed the way to God was through their righteous deeds. Outwardly they had signs of life, but inwardly they were dead. They just didn't get it.

MY LIFE AS A PHARISEE

An occupational hazard of being a pastor is that it is easy to be religious. I get paid to explain, interpret and apply God's law. I go to church almost every day. I read and study the Bible daily. I pray even when I don't want to—at parties, social gatherings, civic functions. I quote Scripture. I answer people's questions about the Bible. I counsel people concerning their problems. I visit the sick, the spiritually lost and the troubled.

I do all these things, but at times my heart is not in it. I undertake needed activities to keep up my religious façade. I pretend to engage in spiritual disciplines. I put up a front and go through the religious motions. But during those times, I'm more concerned with people's impressions and their approval than I am of engaging my heart with God.

I place rule-keeping over my relationship with Jesus. I emphasize works over grace. I acknowledge that Jesus died for my sins, but what really matters are the seven necessary disciplines for Christian growth. I leave no room for gray areas in my life. I want to be right more than I want to love my neighbor. I grow critical of those who aren't being religious like me. I flaunt my behavior. I think God must be proud to have me on his team.

And all the while I don't get it. I miss the reason Jesus came. I miss his story of freedom and forgiveness. I read Scripture but miss the Savior. I can't seem to see past the lists, the regulations and the disciplines. I'm hitting line drives to the outfield wall, but they are caught. So with head held low I walk off the field of my religiosity with little joy.

CALLING IT LIKE I SEE IT

What I experience during my pharisaical times is what the Pharisees experienced daily. Jesus didn't hold anything back in addressing the weaknesses of the Pharisees, and if I want to be like him, I guess I shouldn't either. The hard thing is that as I look closely at them I see some of their negative traits in myself.

They were legalists. Legalism is the tendency to reduce the measure of one's relationship with God to a set of humanly created rules, which can in turn be used as a standard to measure one's spirituality. It is the belief that God's love and acceptance depend on what we do, not what he has already done. These rules aren't spelled out in Scripture. Often they have been passed down, or they have been dictated to the legalist and have become an obsession to him or her. Legalism becomes a rigid, grim and exacting lifestyle. It works in conjunction with guilt and fear, and flourishes in the drab context of negativism.

This belief was the Pharisees' major problem. They assumed the place of authority in Jewish religion and pushed it to unwarranted extremes. It resulted in illegitimate control over the Jewish people, requiring uniformity, not unity.

The Pharisees taught that faith was an outside job. The measure of one's spirituality was how one acted, the title one carried, the sound of one's prayers, the number of meetings one attended and on and on. It clung to the law at the expense of grace, and to the letter in place of the spirit.

The motive of legalism is fear—the overwhelming sense of not doing enough to merit approval before God. The heart of legalism is pride, placing self above God. The missing ingredient is joy. The talk is good, the walk is right, but the face is downcast. The crush of legalism is suffocation of the spirit. The heart is stone cold because rules mean more than the relationship with Jesus. The consequence of legalism is bondage—a loss of freedom and a loss of vitality. Legalism is religious hyperactivity—continuous rule-keeping without a real relationship.

They were traditionalists. Traditions are singing the national anthem before football games, eating turkey and dressing on Thanksgiving, going to church on Sunday. Traditions are a part of life, and they are both good and necessary.

Traditional*ism* occurs when we make our traditions sacred. The reasons behind the traditions are forgotten, but the traditions are perpetuated. The danger of traditions is that they become worshiped and take precedence over Jesus. The Pharisees placed their traditions over the truth.

A great difference exists between truth and traditions. Warren Wiersbe writes in *The Bible Exposition Commentary*, "Tradition is something *external*, the truth of God is *internal,* in the heart. People obey tradition to please people and gain status, but we obey the Word to please God. Tradition deals with *ritual*, God's truth deals with *reality*. Tradition brings empty words to the lips, but truth penetrates the heart and changes the life. Actually, tradition robs a person of the power of the Word of God."

In the end traditionalism becomes a monster. It creates bondage and dutiful work devoid of joy. That was true for the Pharisees. Their traditions made it difficult for them to see the Savior even when they bumped right into him. Traditions shield our eyes from those things that really matter.

They were judgmental. Cartoon buffoon Homer Simpson hadn't seen his born-again neighbor Maude Flanders for a while.

Frankly, I'm not so sure he missed her. The incessantly sunny demeanor of Maude and her husband, Ned, clearly annoyed him.

Yet when Homer saw Maude in her backyard, he greeted her warmly. "I haven't seen you around in a couple of weeks," he said. "Where have you been?"

"Oh," Maude replied cheerily, "I've been away at a Bible camp—learning how to be more judgmental."

Unfortunately, that's what a lot of people think about Christians these days. If you look at Homer's Bible-thumping neighbors, you see a religion that's rigid and superficial, pushy and moralistic, rule-keeping and opinionated.

Sheldon Vanauken was right. In *A Severe Mercy* he says: "The best argument for Christianity is Christians; their joy, their certainty, their completeness. But the strongest argument against Christianity is also Christians—when they are somber and joyless, when they are self-righteous and smug in complacent consecration, when they are narrow and repressive, then Christianity dies a thousand deaths."

The Pharisees were notorious for having a judgmental attitude. They judged Jesus' words, his practice, his belief and his very manner of life. They judged him based on their opinions and their traditions. Whatever did not measure up to their standards and criteria felt the scorn of their ridicule and the butt of their rebuke.

They were hypocritical. "Jesus' constant accusation of the Pharisees was that they were "hypocrite." His most caustic and stirring remarks to the Pharisees came in a longer discourse in Matthew 23. Six times Jesus blasted them, "Woe to you, teachers of the law and Pharisees, you hypocrites!" If that wasn't enough, Jesus also said, "You snakes! You brood of vipers!" (Matthew 23:33). Please don't misunderstand. It was not that Jesus did not love the Pharisees. He did, but he detested their practices. They disgraced the temple, the Scriptures and the Jewish faith, all in the name of God. They were two-faced, religious hypocrites.

The word *hypocrite* comes from the theater. Hypocrites are stage actors. Acting is a noble profession. On the stage, actors lay aside their true identity and assume false ones. They are no longer themselves, but someone else in disguise. In the theater there is no harm or deceit in actors playing their parts. The audience knows that they have come to a drama; they are not taken in by it.

The trouble with religious hypocrites, on the other hand, is that they deliberately set out to deceive people. They take a religious practice and make it a measure of worthiness. They do good deeds and religious activities to earn the applause of God and others.

Hypocrisy strikes such a raw nerve because it is antithetical to what Jesus professed. At the heart of Christianity is authenticity—an authentic relationship with Jesus, authentic relationships with the community of faith, and authentic character of those who claim to be his followers. Hypocrisy is offensive because it pretends to be something authentic; it pretends to be something it is not. Jesus was real. He lived a transparent life. Hypocrisy is false; it seeks to cover up and whitewash, pretending to be something it is not. No wonder it angered Jesus so much.

Pharisees Anonymous

Pharisaism is a kind of addiction. And recovery from any addiction, be it alcohol, drugs, sex or any other, is never complete. Former addicts are never fully outside the risk of succumbing again to their addiction. So to avoid legalism and traditionalism, to completely change a judgmental and hypocritical attitude, is probably impossible.

Alcoholics don't stop being alcoholics; they merely stop drinking. Those with a pharisaical bent stop focusing on rules and start focusing on their relationship with God. This was the point Jesus made to the Pharisees and to his disciples following the Pharisees' question concerning ceremonial cleansing. Jesus brought the conversation back around to the heart of the matter by quoting from the prophet Isaiah: "These people honor me with their lips, but their hearts are far from me" (Matthew 15:8). Then to his disciples he said, "The things that come out of the mouth come from the heart, and these make a man 'unclean' . . . but eating with unwashed hands does not make him 'unclean'" (Matthew 15:18-20). Jesus was instructing his hearers to focus not on the external appearances but on internal reality, to concentrate on the spiritual more than the physical, to emphasize attitudes above actions, to acknowledge grace over works.

Sin has to be dealt with. The Pharisees sought to deal with sin through human endeavor. Jesus dealt with sin by dying for it. Jesus said that the way to heaven comes not by keeping the law, going to church or believing the right doctrine, but through a personal relationship with him. Salvation is God's work, not ours to purchase.

Most of the Pharisees didn't get it. And for a long time, I didn't get it either. But, eventually I did—once I experienced the grace of a loving Lord. The sooner we experience grace the sooner we will get it.

~4~

SEEING SOMEONE
IN THE STORM

Jesus Relieves Our Fear

*I*mmediately Jesus made the disciples get into the boat and go on ahead of him to the other side, while he dismissed the crowd. After he had dismissed them, he went up on a mountainside by himself to pray. When evening came, he was there alone, but the boat was already a considerable distance from land, buffeted by the waves because the wind was against it.

During the fourth watch of the night Jesus went out to them, walk-

ing on the lake. When the disciples saw him walking on the lake, they were terrified. "It's a ghost," they said, and cried out in fear.

But Jesus immediately said to them: "Take courage! It is I. Don't be afraid."

"Lord, if it's you," Peter replied, "tell me to come to you on the water."

"Come," he said.

Then Peter got down out of the boat, walked on the water and came toward Jesus. But when he saw the wind, he was afraid and, beginning to sink, cried out, "Lord, save me!"

Immediately Jesus reached out his hand and caught him. "You of little faith," he said, "why did you doubt?"

And when they climbed into the boat, the wind died down. Then those who were in the boat worshiped him, saying, "Truly you are the Son of God."

When they had crossed over, they landed at Gennesaret. And when the men of that place recognized Jesus, they sent word to all the surrounding country. People brought all their sick to him and begged him to let the sick just touch the edge of his cloak, and all who touched him were healed.

MATTHEW 14:22-36

$\mathcal{A}$ll Americans remember where they were when they heard the news about the terrorist attacks on the World Trade Center in New York and on the Pentagon in Washington, D.C., on September 11, 2001.

I was in Springfield, Illinois, attending the Illinois Baptist State Association Board of Directors' meeting. When the president of the board welcomed the guests, a board member stood to his feet and said, "I've just received word from my wife that a hijacked plane has flown into one of the World Trade Center towers in New York City. It appears to be a terrorist attack. I think we should pray."

The board president agreed. In shocked and stunned silence, we prayed. Then we went on with our meeting. I felt somewhat safe in the Baptist Building in Springfield.

Forty-five minutes later another board member reported, "I work for Scott Air Force base. My secretary just called to inform me that hijacked planes have hit both of the World Trade Center towers. Both are down. And another plane has flown into the Pentagon. I think we need to pray."

Again, the board officers agreed. And again, we prayed.

This time there was more urgency and concern in the voice of the one leading the prayer.

Unable to listen to a radio or watch a television, I sat in the large boardroom with my feelings of shock turning to uncertainty, questioning and fear. *What is going on? How could this be happening? What might be next? When will this stop?* I no longer felt somewhat safe. I was becoming increasingly afraid.

THE FEAR ALARM

In its most common form, fear is an internal warning mechanism signaling danger. It is an internal alarm to take action and remove ourselves from whatever is threatening us. The intensity of our fear is in direct proportion to the immediacy of the danger. What I felt first on the morning of September 11 when I learned of the horrible tragedy was anxiety, a mild form of fear about what was happening, while the people on those planes and in those buildings felt terror, the most extreme degree of fear.

Fear is very much a part of life. It is a God-given emotion. To be afraid is normal. Yet if fear is out of control, it can be the most paralyzing emotion of all. It has the ability to keep people bound in a prison of frustration and hopelessness. It makes people doubt their abilities and paralyzes the free use of their talents.

Fear is not the private domain of the weak. It strikes at the best of us. Fear causes an NBA all-star to miss a free throw in the closing seconds of a game, a successful entrepreneur to escape a budding opportunity for financial gain, a gregarious neighbor to pass on a friendship that could last a lifetime. Fear motivates us to make more money, *just in case*; to always have the resume out, *you never know*; and to look over your shoulder, *you can't trust anyone*. Fear causes grown adults to sleep with a light on. Fear causes people to build fortresses, stockpile food and bury money. Others procrastinate for fear of making the wrong decision. Some scrap good ideas for fear of failure or are scared into playing it safe and refusing to try anything new.

Recently I told my wife that I seem to have two constant emotions: guilt and fear—guilt for not doing enough and fear of doing the wrong things. I've lived with fear most of my life. Maybe it was because of the big old house I grew up in with its squeaks in the floor and cracks when the wind blew that spooked me. Maybe it was because my older brother told me that the bogeyman lived in the attic. Fear is a horrible emotion to live with.

FEAR COMES FACE TO FACE WITH FAITH

Simon Peter was fearful one night in a boat on the Sea of Galilee. Jesus had just fed five thousand people. Peter and his buddies were sailing across the sea at Jesus' request when a tumultuous storm came raging upon them.

A tremendous fear rose up within Peter and the others. Peter was an experienced fisherman who earned his livelihood on the lake. When he became afraid, he had reason to be afraid. A difference exists between imagined fears, phobias that paralyze us, and the real realities of human existence. This storm was real. The rain blasted his face, the wind pierced his skin and the sea filled his boat. This tough fisherman knew that death was imminent. Hope was fleeting with the sinking boat.

At the fourth watch of the night, between 3 and 6 a.m., the disciples saw something approaching their boat. At first it was just a shape to which they paid little attention. As it got closer they finally could see that it was a person walking toward the boat on nothing but the sea itself.

Peter rubbed his eyes. He did a double take. *This can't be real. People can't walk on water. It must be a ghost!*

He and his friends began to cry out in fear. Above the slapping of the wind and the thunder of the waves, their terrified voices pierced the air. While unsure of what was coming toward them, they were confident that they would never see dry land or the light of day again. Peter, initially afraid of the waves, now was terrified of the man walking on the sea.

But this was no ordinary man. It was Jesus. When Jesus came to the disciples on the water, he wasn't performing a neat trick or trying to impress them with his water-walking ability. He was revealing the divine presence and power of God.

Matthew probably recorded the place (Sea of Galilee) and the time (the fourth watch of the night) and the conditions (a storm) to remind us that Jesus often comes when we least expect him. Jesus came when hope was gone, when human ability had failed. Is it coincidental that God often crosses our paths when we have exhausted our limits?

Then Jesus spoke, "Take courage! It is I. Don't be afraid" (Matthew 14:27). His simple words comforted and relieved their fears.

The disciples must have been thinking, *We're saved. Jesus is here. Like he has done before, he will calm the storm. He'll get in the boat with us. And we will sail to the shore so we can put on dry clothes.* But the storm still raged.

Peter piped up. The other men must have thought, *Why can't he leave good enough alone?* "Lord, if it's you, tell me to come to you on the water" (Matthew 14:28). Peter was not testing Jesus; he was pleading with him. Stepping out of the boat was not a logical act; it was a desperate act.

Why would Peter make such a request? Perhaps he thought that since he was going to die, he might as well die with Jesus. Or maybe his fear aroused so much adrenaline that he was compelled toward the heroic. Notice that Peter did not ask for a guarantee of safety or a promise of security; he simply requested an opportunity to walk on water.

Water for a Palestinian in Jesus' day was something for drinking, bathing, and fishing, but not for playing. The people had a healthy respect for water. When Peter asked permission to stroll on the water, did he calculate the consequences? Did he stop to think that human beings don't walk on water?

Peter knew something crucial: the water was where Jesus was, though it was dark, wet and dangerous. For Peter to walk on the water, he had to get out of the boat. To be with Jesus, Peter had to leave his security.

Peter stepped onto the water. It was secure and firm as he walked toward Jesus. Peter really walked. *All right! But wait, this is not right. I can't walk on water.* Peter looked away from Jesus. He saw the waves and felt the wind. Fear took over again. He began to sink, yet he had the presence of mind to call for help. And Jesus reached out and rescued him.

Courage got Peter out of the boat. Faith held him up. Walking on the water hinged on whether he was focused on the Savior or on the storm. The requirements haven't changed.

LIVING A LIFE OF FAITH

I try to construct a manageable life with some security and predictability to maintain the illusion that I am in control. I desire to stay in the boat of my making because it is convenient, safe and warm. And then, something happens—like the tragedy of September 11—to shake everything up. Then I am left with the option to fear the events of this world or focus on the Savior.

I want to be like Peter walking on water. I want to look beyond the reasons for being afraid and see the Savior. I want to move past my fear to live a life of faith. I can't instruct you on how to walk on water. Only Jesus can do that. I can tell you, however, how to get out of the boat. It has to do with our focus.

When we focus on the Savior, we are given courage. Before Jesus said anything about fear or faith to Peter he instructed him, "Take courage!" (Matthew 14:27).

Courage is not the absence of fear, but the ability to walk on in spite of it. Courage is the muscle of character that flexes to give individuals, families and nations strength to continue in the midst of overwhelming odds.

Courage kept firemen and rescue workers searching for bodies amid the wreckage of the World Trade Center and the Pentagon. It gave federal agents the resolve to apprehend possible assassins. It enabled our military personnel to face a cowardly enemy with no regard for human life. It was the strength that surfaced in victims' families to face another day without their loved ones.

Courage enabled me to face a congregation on Wednesday evening following the tragedy on Tuesday. People wanted answers. Where was God? How could he let something like this happen? As their pastor I had to stand in the pulpit, face my people and provide hope and answers. Without courage I would have stayed home.

Several important biblical characters displayed courage. Moses used it when he stood against Pharaoh and refused to be intimidated. Elijah evidenced it when he faced the prophets of Baal on Mount Carmel. David had it when he grabbed his sling in the Valley of Elah to fight the giant Goliath. Daniel demonstrated it when he refused to worship Nebuchadnezzar's statue in Babylon. Job showed it when he was covered with boils and surrounded by misunderstanding. Peter evidenced it when he got out of the boat in the midst of the storm to walk toward Jesus.

It is impossible to survive the storms and calamities of life without courage. Exterior supports may temporarily sustain us, but only inward character creates courage.

But, to get out of the boat, more than courage is needed.

When we focus on the Savior, we sense his commanding presence. When Jesus told Peter, "It is I," he wasn't simply saying, "It's me, Jesus." English translators have added a word to the Greek text: I am *he*. It is *I*. But Matthew used the Greek version of the great, mysterious, self-revealed name of God: "I AM WHO I AM . . . I AM has sent me to you" (Exodus 3:14). Jesus was making the claim that he was God. This was no mere man out for a stroll. He was divinity personified. He was making a statement to his disciples, then and now.

As God, his presence is bigger than any storm or tragedy. We need not forget that. It is easy to take our focus off Jesus when storms strike. Disease is real, disasters happen, death is certain. Storms are big, but God is bigger.

When I stood before my congregation the Sunday following September 11, I reminded them that how we face life is determined not by the size of the storm but by the size of our Savior. If we believe that God is wimpy, we will be fearful. If we think that God is a grandfather, we will be timid. But if our God is the competent, all-powerful God, we can walk forward in faith.

Several years ago J. B. Phillips wrote a book that depicts what many people believe about God. In his book *Your God Is Too Small,* Phillips warns of the dangers of putting God in a box, thereby limiting him to our preconceived notions of who and what he is.

How big is your God? Let's not reduce God to a manageable size. Let's not whittle Jesus down to a mere extension of ourselves. Let's not get so buddy-buddy with him that we lose the grandeur of his personhood. Let's not think God is small because tragedy strikes. He is the God of all creation.

Peter's God was big. His great God was walking before him. Like a powerful headlight that cut through the darkness of the fog, he provided direction and guidance. Peter followed the light of God's presence. He was able to see where to take the next step.

When we focus on the Savior we can walk on in spite of our fear. What would you guess is the most common command in Scripture? "Fear not." The words appear 365 times in the Bible. Like a daily vitamin, God has provided just what we need to conquer daily dreads. This was the encouragement Jesus uttered to Peter.

Once, when I was facing a decision that involved considerable risk, I went to a trusted friend who was much older and wiser than I.

"I'd go ahead," I said, full of stress, "if I were *sure* I could swing it. But . . ."

He looked at me for a moment; then he turned his nameplate on his desk around. He pushed it toward me. There, on a piece of paper taped to the back of the nameplate, were ten handwritten words: "Be bold—and mighty forces will come to your aid."

Boldness means deliberately deciding to walk on in spite of fear, knowing that mighty forces, both physical and spiritual, will assist one in the venture.

Long ago a loving God said to a general, Joshua, who was about to lead his people into the most extensive battle of his life, "Yes, be bold and strong! Banish fear and doubt! For remember, the Lord your God is with you wherever you go" (Joshua 1:9 LB). And Jesus uttered the same thought to Peter who was in a boat fearing for his life: "Take courage! It is I. Don't be afraid" (Matthew 14:27).

When we focus on the Savior we are given the faith to trust. At the climax of the movie *Indiana Jones and the Last Crusade*, Jones has to pass three difficult tests to reach the Holy Grail and save his father, who is dying. The first test is "the Breath of God." As he walks down a corridor, Jones must bow down at precisely the right moment to keep from having his head cut off by large, revolving metal blades. The second test is "the Word of God." Jones must step on just the right stones—the ones that spell God's name in Latin—to keep from falling through the floor to his death.

But the third test, "the Path of God," is the most difficult. Jones comes to the edge of a large chasm—about a hundred feet across and a thousand feet down. On the other side of the chasm is the doorway to the Holy Grail. The instructions say, "Only in the leap from the lion's head will he prove his worth."

Jones says to himself, *It's impossible. Nobody can jump this.* Then he realizes that this test requires a leap of faith. His father says, "You must believe, boy. You must believe!" Even though every nerve and fiber of his being screams that he must not do it, Jones walks to the edge of the cliff, lifts his foot, then steps out into thin air—hoping that somehow he won't splatter on the bottom. He does not plummet to his death, but is upheld by an invisible force.

Likewise, an invisible force held Peter up as he walked toward Jesus. Did he have perfect certainty that he could do it? Probably not. Did he still have doubts? You bet. But he did have enough faith to take a step. He needed only a little faith to put his life on the line. Looking at Jesus gave him faith in faith, the ability to trust the water-walker.

We need that same faith in facing the crises and storms today, faith based on the person and promise of Jesus.

The events following September 11 taught me to trust a loving Savior. Jesus passed by that day. Many people did not see him because of the flames and the debris. Some did not see him because of hatred and prejudice. Others did not see him because their pain and fear were too great. But those who saw him and trusted him were upheld by an invisible force, the same that supported Peter on the Sea of Galilee.

That same force will support us when we face crisis, fear and tragedy.

5

MADMAN TURNED MISSIONARY

Jesus Removes Our Demons

*T*hey sailed to the region of the Gerasenes, which is across the lake from Galilee. When Jesus stepped ashore, he was met by a demon-possessed man from the town. For a long time this man had not worn clothes or lived in a house, but had lived in the tombs. When he saw Jesus, he cried out and fell at his feet, shouting at the top of his voice, "What do you want with me, Jesus, Son of the Most High God? I beg you, don't torture me!" For Jesus had commanded the evil spirit to come out of the man. Many times it had seized him, and though he was chained hand and foot and kept under guard, he had broken his chains and had been driven by the demon into solitary places.

Jesus asked him, "What is your name?"

"Legion," he replied, because many demons had gone into him. And they begged him repeatedly not to order them to go into the Abyss.

A large herd of pigs was feeding there on the hillside. The demons begged Jesus to let them go into them, and he gave them permission. When the demons came out of the man, they went into the pigs, and the herd rushed down the steep bank into the lake and was drowned.

When those tending the pigs saw what had happened, they ran off and reported this in the town and countryside, and the people went out to see what had happened. When they came to Jesus, they found the man from whom the demons had gone out, sitting at Jesus' feet, dressed and in his right mind; and they were afraid. Those who had seen it told the people how the demon-possessed man had been cured. Then all the people of the region of the Gerasenes asked Jesus to leave them, be-

cause they were overcome with fear. So he got into the boat and left.

The man from whom the demons had gone out begged to go with him, but Jesus sent him away, saying, "Return home and tell how much God has done for you." So the man went away and told all over town how much Jesus had done for him.

LUKE 8:26-39

*N*o one wanted anything to do with the man. He was a deranged, dangerous, demon-possessed madman. The foul forces of Satan had driven him to violence. He would cry out like a wild dog howling at the moon. The caves among the tombs of a cemetery were his home.

His family did not know what to do with him. Society did not know how to cure him, so they bound him with chains. But he broke the chains. He ripped off his clothes and cut himself with rocks. He was like a rabid dog on the loose, a menace to society. No one loved him. No one wanted him—except Jesus.

Jesus looked beyond the crazed eyes, the matted hair, the filthy skin, the bloody wrists, the foul smell, the self-inflicted wounds and the ranting and raving. Jesus saw a man in need of a Savior, a broken soul in need of restoration.

The meeting took place in Gerasenes, seven-and-a-half miles across the lake from Galilee. The Hellenistic cities of the Decapolis occupied this area. Alexander the Great had founded these cities in an attempt to plant Greek paganism around the world. This area had long been considered evil. The people living here now were descendants of the despised worshipers of Baal. The residents of the Decapolis had perverted sexual practices, offered child sacrifices and practiced Asherah worship. They sacrificed pigs to their god—pigs, the symbol of evil. This side was the home of pagans, pigs, Gentiles—and Romans, no less. No wonder they were thought to be possessed by demons.

But Jesus came to Gerasenes. His actions were controversial to say the least. No Jewish rabbi would be caught dead on the other side of the lake, nor be involved with Gentile pagans, especially a demoniac one. But Jesus had a mission. Jesus had a reason—a lunatic man that everyone else feared.

Into the region of evil Jesus came. En route, you recall, Jesus calmed a storm. He was demonstrating for his disciples that he was a God who had power over the natural world. Now he would show them that he had power over the supernatural world. His disciples would observe firsthand that he could calm a tormented soul as easily as he calmed a tumultuous sea.

Jesus stepped off the boat and encountered this demon-possessed man in a graveyard with a herd of pigs nearby; both were ritually and culturally unclean for Jews. Out of a cave the wild man ran toward the boat, arms flailing and voice screaming. The disciples must have said, "Jesus, don't you think we'd better get back in the boat and return home? Don't you see that madman coming toward us? He's going to kill us. Jesus, come on, let's get back in the boat." They were horrified, but Jesus wasn't. Jesus wanted this man back.

The disciples were stepping back into the boat while Jesus stood his ground. And instead of attacking Jesus, the madman fell at Jesus' feet like a slave before his master. Jesus ordered the evil spirits out of him. The madman screamed at Jesus, "What do you want with me, Jesus, Son of the Most High God?" (Luke 8:28). The forces of evil could not deny Jesus' identity.

Jesus asked, "What is your name?" (Luke 8:30).

"Legion," he replied in a raspy voice.

A Roman legion was six thousand men strong. The demonic force stationed within this man's soul was formidable, but in the presence of Jesus they cowered away. Instead of being sent into the abyss, the demons requested to be exorcised into the herd of pigs. Though the demons had reaped fear and havoc in a region, they begged for mercy from Jesus. His presence reduced them to groveling weaklings.

Jesus granted their request. They threw themselves into the herd of swine. Immediately the possessed pigs rushed headlong over the cliffs and into the waiting sea below, where the entire herd died.

What society could not do in years Jesus did in an instant. He transformed a lunatic. He rescued a fallen person. He set free a prisoner. He made a madman sane.

But the story did not end there. The pig herders stampeded into town and told the pig farmers what had happened. Out came the pig farmers, and they were angry. Their livelihood, not to mention their food supply, was destroyed. When they ventured out to the grassy knoll near the graveyard where the pigs had been, "they found the man from whom the demons had gone out, sitting at Jesus' feet, dressed and in his right mind; and they were afraid" (Luke 8:35).

Why? Were they more afraid of the deliverer than the demon-possessed man? Did they value pigs more than the presence of God? Did they sense the wonder of a miracle and become frightened by the miracle worker? Or did they prefer yesterday's traditions over today's living God?

What a tragedy. The Savior had crossed their paths. He was ready to heal the sick, to forgive sins, to proclaim the good news of the gospel and to cast out demons, but all the people sent him away. How many lives went unchanged, how many sick went unhealed, how many captives went unreleased because a herd of swine was judged more valuable than a human soul?

Jesus never stayed where he was not welcomed. He stepped back onto the boat from which he came. The possessed man begged to go with Jesus. While the disciples were trying to understand the storm-calming work and soul-freeing power of Jesus, the madman formerly known as Legion knew he was in the presence of God. He wanted to be with him always. He asked for permission to go with Jesus, but Jesus gave him a different mission. "Return home and tell how much God has done for you" (Luke 8:39). Start at your home, tell the entire city and then all the cities of the Decapolis how the Savior has touched you and made you whole.

Crossing the path of the Savior changed this man's life forever. Jesus met him in a cemetery, pulled him from the darkness of a tomb, dressed him in his right mind, set him free and sent him home with a message.

CAN WE BE RESTORED?

In an earlier version, the nursery rhyme "Humpty Dumpty" was a riddle. It asked the question, "What, when broken, can never be repaired, not even by strong or wise individuals?" As any child knows, the answer is an egg. Regardless of how hard we try, a broken egg can never be put back together again. We simply have to learn to live with the mess.

The demoniac was like Humpty Dumpty, a broken egg, with no hope of being put together again. He was downcast and dejected. He had tasted defeat and felt the pain of brokenness.

Like Humpty Dumpty and the madman of Gerasenes, we fall. We flail around with fatigue, frustrations, failure and fears; we are beat up by discouragement, depression and despair; we are broken with battle scars, open wounds and emotional pain; we are helpless and confused. Jesus wants to restore our souls. We need his help to get back up again. We need a Savior, one who will cross our paths and pick us up and make us whole.

Jesus searches for us, comforts us, reassures us and sets us free. He did it for the demoniac, and he will do it for us. No matter how far we have fallen, we can be raised. No matter how tattered our life, it can be repaired. Unlike the king's horses and the king's men, God can put us together again.

JESUS UNCHAINED HIM TO USE HIM

The engagement this man had with Jesus could be described as a head-on collision: the kingdom of darkness clashing with the kingdom of light. It was highly charged, an emotional encounter. In this meeting the demon-possessed man experienced the power of Jesus. When he crossed paths with the Savior, Jesus left some indelible marks.

Jesus met him. The demoniac was a damned man—forgotten and alone. Jesus battled a storm on the sea and rowed seven-and-a-half miles to the region of the damned.

"The other side" was outside of the disciples' comfort zone. But Jesus engaged this madman on his turf, in an area where the people did not look, dress, act, talk or think like Jews. Gerasenes was a cesspool for human depravity. It was a place of moral and ethical decay. It was a place where sin was rampant and death was a stench on people's clothes. But Jesus still went there to meet the demoniac.

The next time I feel beyond Jesus' reach, or I see people around me as beyond his reach, I will remember the lengths he went to in order to save a madman from destruction. If he was willing to do it then, he is willing to do it now. No matter how far we have fallen, or how desperate we are, Jesus is ready and willing to meet us.

Jesus cured him. The demoniac was a sick man tormented in body and mind. When Jesus came the demons knew they were goners, but they made a request. They asked to go into the swine rather than be destroyed in the Abyss. Why did Jesus send the demons into the pigs rather than into hell? The most plausible answer to this question is that the demon-infested swine became a witness that the former madman was indeed healed. If Christ had sent the demons directly back to hell, the world would have looked the same, and the man would have had no visible evidence that the demons were really gone. Jesus sent the demons into the pigs not to be kind to the demons, but to be kind to the demoniac. The pigs at the bottom of the cliffs were reminders of God's complete healing.

Jesus freed him. The demoniac was a bound man—physically and spiritually enslaved.

His demons were no different than the demons that make us feel unworthy because of past mistakes or the demons that make us feel unclean because we have broken one of the commandments or the demons that burden us with guilt or the demons that nag us because we fail to live up to others' expectations.

The cures of the madman's culture were restriction and isolation. Jesus, on the other hand, crossed his path and exposed the demoniac to acceptance and love. This is what drove the madman to his knees. Hatred imprisoned him. Love set him free to health and life.

Jesus, the liberator, strips the chains from our ankles and wrists, drives the demons out and frees us to understand the good news: Jesus has accepted us. To hear the liberating word is a shattering experience, for it is something totally new. It is like a deaf person hearing a symphony for the first time or a blind person finally seeing the splendor of the Grand Canyon.

What Jesus did for the demoniac, he can do for us. Scripture reminds us that Jesus "loves us and has freed us from our sins by his blood" (Revelation 1:5). The most basic truth of Christianity is that Jesus Christ has already paid for all of our sins, past, present and future. No psychologist or preacher can free us from our sin; only Jesus can do that. Ultimately all sin is against him. Because of Jesus' sacrifice on the cross, God forgives our sin and guilt and frees us to live again.

Jesus restored him. The demoniac was a useless man—unfit and destructive. The demons had torn him up and driven him down. His was a wasted life.

Satan does that to people: he steals and destroys life. Jesus, on the other hand, restores people to health, hope and usefulness.

Because of the encounter with Jesus, this man who was once self-destructive became self-controlled. Once naked and intimidating, he became clothed and gentle. Once isolated from people, he became integrated into society. Once mentally and spiritually tormented, he came into his right mind. Once destined for hell, he became a child of heaven.

It took years for Satan to whittle this man's life down to such a tormented state; it took Jesus moments to restore it. His desire is to give back what Satan has stolen. His plan is to fix what the enemy has broken.

Restoration is not a solo event. It requires the strength and refashioning of another. Sometimes the restoration that Jesus offers comes in practical ways through the help of a support group, a Bible study class, a pastor or a trained counselor. These people can be the face of God, reminding the broken and wounded that they are valuable to God and to society.

Jesus commissioned him. The demoniac was a purposeless man—with no calling or direction. His life was merely a day-to-day existence with little future or hope.

Jesus changed all of that. He gave him a mission. "Return home and tell how much God has done for you" (Luke 8:39). He was a madman turned missionary, delivering the greatest message of all.

What I like about him was that he understood the lesson Jesus was demonstrating to his disciples. He realized that Jesus was God. Notice the terminology shift. Jesus instructed the man to "tell how much *God* has done for you," and he went away and "told all over town how much *Jesus* had done for him" (Luke 8:39, emphasis added).

Yes, Jesus restored him, but not merely to make him a model citizen. He restored him to fulfill a purpose. The word *restore* was used in biblical times to describe the mending of a fisherman's nets in order to be used the next day. The man was mended so he could accomplish a purpose for which he was intended. He now had the greatest reason to live.

If you are living with a sense of desperation, if your life has been marred by Satan's invasion, if a certain sin is so deeply rooted that deliverance seems impossible, if you have given up on your future, let me remind you that if Jesus could restore a madman living in a graveyard and turn him into a missionary, he can restore you.

6

CATCHING OUR
REFLECTION IN
THE WATER

Jesus Cleanses Our Past

*W*hen a Samaritan woman came to draw water, Jesus said to her, "Will you give me a drink?" (His disciples had gone into the town to buy food.)

The Samaritan woman said to him, "You are a Jew and I am a Samaritan woman. How can you ask me for a drink?" (For Jews do not associate with Samaritans.)

Jesus answered her, "If you knew the gift of God and who it is that asks you for a drink, you would have asked him and he would have given you living water."

"Sir," the woman said, "you have nothing to draw with and the well is deep. Where can you get this living water? Are you greater than our father Jacob, who gave us the well and drank from it himself, as did also his sons and his flocks and herds?"

Jesus answered, "Everyone who drinks this water will be thirsty again, but whoever drinks the water I give him will never thirst. Indeed, the water I give him will become in him a spring of water welling up to eternal life."

The woman said to him, "Sir, give me this water so that I won't get thirsty and have to keep coming here to draw water."

He told her, "Go, call your husband and come back."

"I have no husband," she replied.

Jesus said to her, "You are right when you say you have no husband. The fact is, you have had five husbands, and the man you now have is not your husband. What you have just said is quite true."

"Sir," the woman said, "I can see that you are a prophet. . . . I know that Messiah" (called Christ) *"is coming. When he*

comes, he will explain everything to us."

Then Jesus declared, "I who speak to you am he." . . .

Then, leaving her water jar, the woman went back to the town and said to the people, "Come, see a man who told me everything I ever did. Could this be the Christ?" They came out of the town and made their way toward him. . . .

Many of the Samaritans from that town believed in him because of the woman's testimony, "He told me everything I ever did." So when the Samaritans came to him, they urged him to stay with them, and he stayed two days. And because of his words many more became believers.

JOHN 4:7-41

*W*ould it be a blessing to erase our past? Are there some events and mistakes that we would like to forget? Everyone has a story. If we have lived long enough we have a past. Many of us would like to erase our past errors and mishaps. I would. So would a woman who lived in Sychar, Samaria, during Jesus' day.

THE STORY OF A TROUBLED PAST

The apostle John told her story. She was not given a name, just referred to as the Samaritan woman. Samaria was that section of real estate sandwiched between Galilee to the north and Judea to the south in Israel. The people who lived there were half-breeds. They had intermarried with the Assyrians. They had their own place of worship, Mount Gerizim, because the Jews refused to let them worship in the temple at Jerusalem. To put it mildly, they were hated by the Jews.

Yet Jesus traveled through Samaria rather than taking the more customary route east of the Jordan River through Perea. "He had to go through Samaria" (John 4:4). And this woman was the reason.

She had a divine appointment to keep. Little did she know that she would see a Savior who would radically impact her life.

It was high noon. The sun was at its peak and this day was a scorcher. She strolled through the heat on the rocky path to the well known as Jacob's well. She carried an empty jar to fill. While the other women came early in the day, to avoid the heat and to engage in conversation, she came at midday to avoid their scorn and stares. She always arrived alone.

Her heart was as heavy as the water jar she toted. Her soul was as empty as its contents. Her spirit was as dry as the dust that stirred from her sandals. She pondered the futile road she had wandered. She retraced the roads she might have taken and the happiness she might have found. But her mind echoed the words, *What's done is done. You can't go back. You can't relive the past: failed relationships, empty promises and bad choices.* She had ventured down one path after another seeking fulfillment, and each time she had lowered her bucket hoping to quench her thirst for love and meaning, she had come up empty and disappointed.

The empty water jar was a fit reminder of her life.

A man was sitting by the well. A Jewish man. And he really saw her. He looked beyond her appearance and her pretension to see the hurt of her heart, the hollowness of her soul and the aridity of her spirit. He spoke to her. He offered her water—himself, the living water. Only he could soothe the hurt, fill the soul and quench the spirit.

Jesus knew her past. "You have had five husbands, and the man you now have is not your husband" (John 4:18). *How did he know? Had he been this way before? Had he asked someone?* He stated her past and current marital status. But he did not call her a sinner. (Never did Jesus call anyone a sinner. He did call some people snakes and vipers, but he never called anyone a sinner.) He gave no evangelistic appeal. He presented no structured plan of salvation. He didn't even pray with her.

Here was the Savior of the world conversing with a Samaritan adulteress. He was giving her the opportunity to move beyond her checkered past by offering her the gift of all gifts. All those years she had given of herself—her virginity, her morality, her self-respect, her value—all in the hope of finding what this man offered her.

Jesus looked beyond her past performance and saw her value as a person. He offered compassion instead of condemnation. Jesus walked into her life when most people walked out. This was one of the most appealing and comforting characteristics of Jesus. He traveled into places where others dared not. He talked with people that others would not. And he gave satisfaction—living water—that others could not.

In a moment, she was cleansed and freed. The guilt of her sin was removed. The chains of her past were broken. The barrenness of her soul sprang to life like a parched desert after a downpour. She began to bubble like a mountain brook. The joy and enthusiasm of her forgiven heart overflowed.

Her newfound life couldn't be contained. She had to tell someone. She ran to the women that had shunned her and the men that had used her. She hurried off to tell them about the man who "told me everything I ever did" (John 4:29). She's received from Jesus everything that she wanted and needed.

HER STORY IS OUR STORY

Like the jar of the woman at the well, our jars are empty too. Some of us achieve success and status, others languish in the valleys of failure and defeat, still others are entrenched somewhere in between. Regardless of the position, our souls are dreadfully empty.

I recall a lunch conversation with a successful businessman who expressed just this sort of inner emptiness. His face was etched with pain as he told the story of his troubled past. I'll never forget his words: "I peer into the reflection of myself as I polish the car, or stare at the nameplate on my desk. All I can see is the hurt and pain of decisions that I have made and the lost opportunities for happiness that I have forfeited. I know that I can never go back."

And I realize that I am not much different. Only the circumstances have changed. I would love to retrieve a verbalized thought, correct a sordid mistake, take a different road, or undo a destructive event.

Like the businessman, we need a new start, a fresh beginning. We desperately desire a cleansing, something or someone who will take away the sting of past memories. We want to have our souls filled with the cleansing and purifying water of God's love so we can run down a new path.

AN INVENTORY OF THE PAST

But something keeps popping up. It's our past—a conglomeration of dreams, plans, successes and failures that makes us who we are because of what we have done. Our past is filled with disappointments and delights. For many of us the personal inventory of past failures overshadows any hope of future fulfillment.

The past haunts us. Like the Samaritan woman who heard the taunts and the innuendoes, we hear sharp and damning remarks from people we deeply love and respect. My father, in a fit of rage, once said to me as a child, "You're no good; you'll never amount to anything." For years those words haunted me, and even now some of my work ethic is my effort to defeat those words said only once in a fit of anger. Proverbs states, "Reckless words pierce like a sword" (12:18). Wounding words are like a bullet lodged in our body and hidden under our skin. We can't see it, but we can feel it.

While some people can't get out of their minds the painful remarks made by others in their past, some can't escape the memories of foolish acts. The Samaritan woman's journey down the wrong path may have begun with a seemingly innocent tryst with her boyfriend. But the romance went too far and now she bears the consequences forever. For others it may be an impulse to move outside the boundaries of the law. Still others, on a dare from friends, do a foolish and damaging act that can never be corrected.

And now the past mistakes are forever on display. Our thoughtless blunders are hard to hide and even harder to forget. The Psalmist David wrote of his horrible mistake of sleeping with a woman who wasn't his wife and then having her husband killed to cover up his mistake: "For I know my transgressions, / and my sin is always before me" (Psalm 51:3).

At other times we are haunted by our failure to act—a job that wasn't done, a word that wasn't spoken, a letter that wasn't written, a forgiveness that wasn't offered. I suspect that the Samaritan woman recalled every day the path she failed to walk, a path of hope and opportunity that she ignored. Often this same omission is played out in our minds. We might say, "If only I had majored in finance," "If only I had married," "If only I had taken the other job," "If only I had followed God's leading," "If only . . . " We long for a second chance.

The past marks us. We would rather forget some past events, but everywhere we turn they keep popping up, reminding us of what we did. Take Bill Buckner, first baseman for the Boston Red Sox during the 1986 World Series. It was the tenth inning of game six. The Red Sox were leading the series 3-2. If the Red

Sox won this game they would win the World Series. Mookie Wilson of the New York Mets hit a slow-rolling ball to Buckner that would end the inning. It was a routine grounder. Bill Buckner had fielded hundreds of groundballs. The grounder rolled toward Buckner, but slipped between his legs. The Red Sox lost the game and eventually the World Series. From that day forward Bill Buckner, a better-than-average baseball player, would forever be remembered for his error that cost the Red Sox the World Series. On a trip from Chicago to Phoenix I was looking through the airline's magazine that sells stuff that no one really needs. In full color was a still-life image of the ball bouncing through Bill Buckner's legs and Mookie Wilson running toward first base.

How would you like your past mistakes photographed and sold to the general public? The Samaritan woman felt her own shame to the point that she made her way into the public during the scorching heat of the day to avoid reminders of her past.

I'm sure everywhere Bill Buckner goes, even to this day, he is reminded of and remembered for his mistake. So are we in one way or another; our past leaves an indelible mark on our lives.

The past repeats itself. The Samaritan woman had had five husbands. The past for many of us is repeated until it becomes our way of life. Like a stuck recording that repeats the same word of a song, our past reverberates the same wrongful behavior over and over again.

JESUS CLEANSES OUR PAST

But our past does not have to determine our future. What the Savior did for the Samaritan woman, he can do for us. When we allow the love of Jesus to intersect with our lives, he gives us hope for tomorrow and fills the emptiness of our souls. And all the while, Jesus knows our past. He knew the sordidness of the Samaritan woman's, but he spoke to her in spite of it. He knows the mistakes of our past, and he offers us the gift of living water that will cleanse it.

Water is a cleansing agent. We are instructed to drink eight eight-ounce glasses of water each day. We use water to wash our clothes and our cars. The water that Jesus offered to the Samaritan woman was a spiritual rinse to purify and purge the condemning past. By taking this gift she could begin the long journey of recovery away from her past.

At the circus, the trapeze artists swing on their trapezes high above the spectators. As they swing out into the unknown void to do their spins and somersaults they have to let go of one trapeze, hover for a moment in the void, before catching hold of the other trapeze. Trapeze artists cannot retain a grasp of the old bar while groping for the new one. It is only in the releasing of their support, their hold on the past, that they can move forward.

Once we know God is at the end of the other trapeze, we can let go of the past. The Old Testament prophet Isaiah wrote, "This is what the LORD says: . . . 'Forget the former things; do not dwell on the past'" (43:16, 18). God is not implying that we should erase all past memories of family, friends and experiences. He is saying that we need to let go of the past—those habits, fears, mistakes, controlling influences and people that are preventing us from taking a new road to life and health. In other words, we need to release the ties and traditions that prevent us from soaring to a new life. We need to leave behind any encumbrances that keep us from moving on with our lives.

I did not learn to swim until I was eleven years old. I was cautious of water and have been for all of my life. When my wife and I were vacationing in Cancun, Mexico, we decided to go snorkeling. Actually, she decided and I went along. We were taken out to a bay that supposedly had beautiful coral reefs and exotic fish. The water was choppy that day, and I spent more time spitting salt water out of my snorkel than looking at fish. A couple of times waves came over me; in trying to spit out the water from my snorkel, I swallowed it. I thought I was going to drown. I couldn't have been happier when we got back to dry land.

A few years later my wife and I went to Maui, Hawaii. Everyone said, "You have to go snorkeling." A favorite place for snorkeling that locals told us about was just a short walk down the beach from our hotel. Again, my wife wanted to go. I didn't want to go, remembering the near-drowning experience in Cancun, but I complied. We proceeded to water that was peaceful and calm. As we swam out from the shoreline, we saw beneath the water's surface the most spectacular rock formations with the most beautiful fish swimming in all directions. Here's the point: I only experienced the beauty as I let go of my past fears and reluctance. If I had held on to my past memories, I would have never enjoyed some of God's marvelous creations.

The Samaritan woman let go of her past. She based her future not on her past misdeeds, but on the person of Christ. She came face to face with the Savior and placed her life—past, present and future—in his hands. Jesus did not ask her for a commitment, he did not ask her to sign a contract, and he demanded no retribution. He didn't even ask her to repent. He simply sent her on her way with her past behind her and a new future before her. He didn't just give her a new smile; he gave her a new purpose. She wasn't to become merely a container for the living water, but a conduit so that living water would flow to others.

And flow it did. She couldn't stop talking about the Savior that knew everything about her. He had transformed her life. Her future looked bright for the first time in a long while. She could face the new day and the old acquaintances. Her soul was full to overflowing.

A LUNCH,
A HUNGRY CROWD
AND A MIRACLE

Jesus Uses Our Inadequacies

*W*hen Jesus heard what had happened, he withdrew by boat privately to a solitary place. Hearing of this, the crowds followed him on foot from the towns. When Jesus landed and saw a large crowd, he had compassion on them and healed their sick.

As evening approached, the disciples came to him and said, "This is a remote place, and it's already getting late. Send the crowds away, so they can go to the villages and buy themselves some food."

Jesus replied, "They do not need to go away. You give them something to eat."

"We have here only five loaves of bread and two fish," they answered.

"Bring them here to me," he said. And he directed the people to sit down on the grass. Taking the five loaves and the two fish and looking up to heaven, he gave thanks and broke the loaves. Then he gave them to the disciples, and the disciples gave them to the people. They all ate and were satisfied, and the disciples picked up twelve basketfuls of broken pieces that were left over. The number of those who ate was about five thousand men, besides women and children.

MATTHEW 14:13-21

$\mathcal{M}$any years ago a little girl lived in the slums of Philadelphia. One day a pastor started a Sunday school for neighborhood children. This child came to the very first meeting, but the meeting room was small and a number of other children had to be turned away. Hattie May Wyatt went to bed that night unhappy because her less fortunate playmates had no place to hear about Jesus. Always rather weak, Hattie May died two years later and her parents sent for the minister. They handed him a worn, red pocketbook they had found beneath her pillow. In it were exactly fifty-seven pennies and a note scrawled in Hattie May's childish handwriting: "This is to help build the little church bigger so more children can go to Sunday School." For two years this frail child had run errands to help her neighbors. The pennies she had earned had all been carefully saved.

The next Sunday the minister carried the cracked red pocketbook to his pulpit. He took out the fifty-seven pennies and dropped them one by one back into the purse. Then he told about the little girl who gave all she had. The congregation was deeply touched.

Then a miracle took place.

Before we talk about the miracle in Philadelphia, let's talk about a principle: A small amount placed in the right hands can accomplish much. When our giving goes out on a limb it can change the course of history.

THE MIRACLE OF MULTIPLICATION

Such a miracle was witnessed in Bethsaida when a little nameless boy crossed the path of Jesus. It was a demonstration of devotion that would never be forgotten—the miracle of multiplication.

Jesus had gone to Bethsaida on the northeastern side of the Sea of Galilee. Earlier that day Jesus had learned of John the Baptist's death. John was Jesus' cousin, his forerunner, co-worker and friend. John came closer to understanding Jesus than any other person. Now he was dead. Herod had him killed. Jesus' own life was threatened.

Jesus chose to get away for a while. "When Jesus heard what had happened, he withdrew by boat privately to a solitary place" (Matthew 14:13). I can understand Jesus' reasoning, can't you? Hearing the distressing news, he was grieving. He was exhausted. His heart needed a break, his body sought rest, and his soul required replenishment. The people business is very draining and if, at times, those in it don't get away from the demands and pressures, they will experience physical and emotional repercussions. Seeking solitude, Jesus sailed to the other side of the lake.

But once across the lake, Jesus encountered a mass of people. They had followed him. It was a six-mile hike around the northeastern corner of the Sea of Galilee. And now people were cascading out of the hills and villages to hear him. The Gospel writers said there were five thousand men, not including women and children. Some scholars estimated the crowd to be as high as twenty-five thousand. They swarmed around Jesus. Each had individual needs and hurts and pains. These people touched the heart of Jesus. Their needs eclipsed his needs. Matthew said, "He had compassion on them" (Matthew 14:14). Literally, his inner being was stirred. The statement reflects an emotion stronger than sympathy. Jesus saw needy people in need of help, so he healed the sick and taught the masses. Jesus *demonstrated* a sermon through a miracle.

Other than the crucifixion, this event is the only event recorded by all four Gospel writers. Clearly it is important.

Darkness was falling. The markets were closed. The crowd was hungry. The disciples were acutely aware of the predicament of the people. Their solution: send the people away. Jesus' solution: Bring them to me. Jesus was up to something. John, in his account, wrote, "He already had in mind what he was going to do" (John 6:6). Jesus was concerned, compassionate and considerate. He was aware of every detail of life. He did not want to send these people away without feeding them.

The disciples didn't have a clue as to how it could be done. Philip surmised the situation and knew it would take three-quarters of a year's salary to buy bread for this group. Andrew, on the other hand, brought people to Jesus. I'm quite certain that when he brought Peter to Jesus, he had no idea Jesus would look behind the rough exterior of Peter to see not only a Galilean fisherman but one who had in him the makings of the rock on whose confession the church would be founded. Likewise, I'm almost as certain that when Andrew brought a little boy with his lunch to Jesus, he had no idea that Jesus would see in those five loaves of barley bread and two fish enough food to feed a small city of people.

We don't know this boy's name or what he looked like. We know only what he gave: five barley loaves and two small fish, a lunch he probably would have eaten any other day around noon. But not this day. He was caught up with the crowd watching and listening to this man named Jesus.

The boy's lunch for a crowd of 25,000 seemed as insignificant as Hattie May's fifty-seven pennies for a new church building. The boy gave Jesus his lunch. It wasn't much, but it was all that he had.

Then the miracle took place.

Jesus blessed the bread and the small fish that had been given. Understanding that logistics might be a problem—hungry people start riots—Jesus instructed his disciples to assemble the crowd in groups of fifty and one hundred. Then the disciples, like well-trained waiters, delivered the blessed food to the people. The crowd was fed. And the people "all ate and were satisfied" (Matthew 14:20). And if that wasn't miracle enough, Jesus made sure nothing was wasted. The disciples retrieved "twelve basketfuls of broken pieces that were left over" (Matthew 14:20). The disciples looked on in amazement.

When we put a little into the hands of Jesus, he multiplies it. If Jesus can take a boy's lunch to feed a city, he can take our gifts and multiply them. He can take our insufficiencies and make them sufficient. He can make our inadequacies more than adequate for each situation we face.

THE MOTIVATION FOR GIVING

What would motivate a young boy to give his lunch to Jesus? Surely the boy was hungry too. His mother would have expected him to eat it. He had a long journey ahead of him back home. Why did he give all he had? The same reasons he gave the bread are the same reasons we are to give our meager gifts to Jesus.

All of our gifts—small and large—belong to Jesus. I may possess much, but I own nothing. God owns it all. And, therefore, he has the right to whatever he wants whenever he wants it. I don't have rights; I only have responsibilities. The young boy understood that his lunch wasn't his. Sure, his mother made it. It was in his knapsack and in his hands. But if Jesus wanted it, it was his for the taking and his for the using.

The psalmist stated:

> The earth is the LORD's, and everything in it,
>
> the world, and all who live in it. (Psalm 24:1)

Since everything belongs to Jesus, I must hold things loosely in my hands. If I hold onto things too tightly, when Jesus requests them and wants them, it hurts when they are removed from my possession. But when I hold things loosely they slide gently out of my possession when Jesus wants and needs them.

Physical needs compel us to give. Confront Jesus with a lost soul, a tired body or a hungry spirit and his first instinct is to help. This miracle met a human need. Jesus was willing to forgo his personal desires to help those who were hurting around him. So, too, did the boy with the lunch. He, too, recognized the need of the people. The people were hungry and tired. They would be traveling home soon and needed a good meal before embarking.

Hattie May saw a need and she gave. The boy saw a need and he gave. Jesus saw a need and he gave. The heart of giving is a desire to meet people's needs.

God works best when he has something to work with, even if it's just a little thing. The focal point of Jesus' sermon through this miracle was that he could work even when he was given a little. God specializes in multiplying little things into big things. God's power is seen as we give Jesus something with which to work. It matters little what the gift is as long as it is given to Jesus.

Jesus didn't make the bread out of nothing. He didn't multiply thin air into fish. But he did take five loaves and two fish and feed a hungry crowd of twenty-five thousand with twelve baskets of leftovers.

It is difficult for Jesus to bless gifts that are not given. But when we give Jesus our meager rations, he can work a miracle. While our gifts may seem insignificant, once given to God, he can multiply them into abundance. Our part is to be available and generous. His part is to perform the spectacular.

THE MESSAGE OF THE MIRACLE

Andrew brought the little boy with his lunch to Jesus. Holding up his lunch bag, I can hear him say, "Jesus, it's not much, but if you can use it, it's yours." The faithfulness and obedience of a child moved the Master.

What will you do with your lunch?

Do what you can. Jesus asks us to do what we can, and he does the rest. He didn't ask the boy to feed the crowd. All he asked for was his lunch.

Will you do what you can? Don't focus on the abilities you don't have. Jesus wants to know what abilities we have made available to him.

Be faithful in the little things. Some people talk about what they would offer to God if they won the lottery or received a large inheritance. Jesus is not interested in what we would give if we had a windfall of cash. The question is, What are we doing with what we have now? If we are not faithful in the small things, there is no reason to believe that we will be faithful in the big things. If we don't give unselfishly of what we have, there is no reason to believe that we will give of what we might get.

The miracle of Bethsaida hinged on the faithfulness of a little boy and a sack lunch. What if he had not been faithful? What if he had not been willing?

One person can make a difference. History is rich with examples of single individuals who made a lasting impression on the world. Napoleon, when on the battlefield, according to Wellington, was the equivalent of 40,000 soldiers. Winston Churchill breathed hope and courage into a dispirited and frightened nation during World War II. Oscar Schindler saved the lives of hundreds of Jews from Nazi concentration camps. And one little boy fed a crowd because he gave his lunch to Jesus.

Little do we know the impact our life is having on those around us. Jesus can take seemingly insignificant persons and make them significant. That's the message of this miracle. A single person, usable and available to Jesus, can impact the whole world.

The little boy with the lunch didn't miss the miracle. He walked away from that experience a changed person. His heart was full of wonder, but his knapsack was empty. He had experienced the miracle of multiplication: A small amount placed in the right hands can be transformed into much.

This brings me back to Hattie May, the frail little girl who worked and saved and gave her fifty-seven pennies to build a bigger church so her friends could hear about Jesus.

Following the minister's graphic display of dropping the pennies back into the purse on the Sunday following her death, a guest came forward and offered some very desirable land for a new church building saying, "I will let the church have it for a fraction of its value. The down payment is exactly fifty-seven pennies."

When the story was told in the newspapers, checks came in from far and wide. Today the Temple Baptist Church impresses visitors to Philadelphia with a seating capacity of 3,300. Its Sunday school building is large enough to accommodate every child who wants to attend. And it all began with a little girl who unselfishly gave all she had.

~8~

AN EXTRAORDINARY
FUNERAL

Jesus Feels Our Pain

Soon afterward, Jesus went to a town called Nain, and his disciples and a large crowd went along with him. As he approached the town gate, a dead person was being carried out—the only son of his mother, and she was a widow. And a large crowd from the town was with her. When the Lord saw her, his heart went out to her and he said, "Don't cry."

Then he went up and touched the coffin, and those carrying it stood still. He said, "Young man, I say to you, get up!" The dead man sat up and began to talk, and Jesus gave him back to his mother.

They were all filled with awe and praised God. "A great prophet has appeared among us," they said. "God has come to help his people." This news about Jesus spread throughout Judea and the surrounding country.

LUKE 7:11-17

*F*ranklin Pierce seemed well equipped for the responsibilities of the presidency of the United States: he was well educated, spoke effectively, had a commanding appearance and exuded charm and honesty. His piety extended to his daily living. Everyone predicted he would perform brilliantly when he took office. Few presidencies, however, have failed more dismally.

Eight weeks before his inauguration, Franklin and Jane Pierce and their one living child, Benny, were traveling by train when the carelessness of a drunken brakeman caused an accident. The parents were only slightly injured, but Benny was caught in the wreckage and died. Ironically, the president-elect's son was the only fatality of the accident. Jane and Franklin Pierce were devastated.

When the Pierces arrived in Washington a few weeks later, they asked that the usual inaugural festivities not be held. Mrs. Pierce continued to wear black mourning clothes for the entire four years her husband held office. Franklin Pierce also seemed to continue to live under a cloud of bereavement. He began to drink heavily to try to numb the feelings of grief over Benny's death. His presidency suffered.

Rejected for a second term because of his ineffectiveness, Pierce and his wife left the White House to return to New Hampshire. Their lives continued to be unhappy. The death of their son was such an offense to the Pierces that they wallowed helplessly in grief.

Death always seems offensive. The finality of death, especially the death of a child, seems unacceptable. The death of someone you love hurts greatly. And the death of a child is among the most painful of all death experiences. When parents die, a large part of the past dies; when a child dies, a part of the future dies. Those left behind often find it difficult to talk about these feelings. Often we feel like no one cares—especially God.

WHEN DEATH PAYS A VISIT

One such person who felt that way was a lady who lived in a small village named Nain. Nain was located twenty-five miles southwest of Capernaum, six miles from Nazareth. It was one of thousands of little villages dotting the landscape of Israel. No major events or breaking news stories ever occurred here.

Why did Jesus travel to Nain? What was his itinerary that day?

Approaching the outskirts of the city, the crowd with Jesus met a funeral procession coming out of the city. What a contrast! Jesus and his disciples were rejoicing in the blessings of the Lord, but the funeral folk were lamenting the loss of a loved one.

Funerals were big business and honored traditions in Jesus' day. Often, professional mourners were hired to cry and wail, drawing attention to the procession. Bystanders were expected to join in the procession. The family's mourning would continue for thirty days.

This procession was especially mournful, for the "dead person was . . . the only son of his mother, and she was a widow"

(Luke 7:12). The woman had lost her husband, and now her only son, her last means of support, was dead. The crowd of mourners would go home and she would be left alone. Her future looked bleak. She would likely be forced to beg for food.

The funeral service was over. The burial was next. Ahead of this woman walked the men carrying the body of her son, her only son, on a stretcher.

Numb with sorrow, she scuffled along. Tears were flowing, interrupted only by piercing wails. All she could do was stare at the back of the stretcher in front of her.

Suddenly the pallbearers stopped. She stopped. The procession stopped.

A man had stepped in front of the them. The widow did not know him. He wasn't at the funeral. She had no idea what he was doing. But before the woman could object, he raised his hand and spoke to her, "Don't cry" (Luke 7:13).

Don't cry? Don't cry! This is a funeral. My son is dead. Don't cry? You are supposed to cry at funerals. Who are you anyway to tell me not to cry? These were her thoughts, but before she stated them, the unknown man acted.

He came to the stretcher where her son was lying. He touched it and spoke: "Young man, I say to you, get up!" (Luke 7:14).

"Wait just a minute. Who are you to say such a thing? You can't . . ." one of the pallbearers objected. But a sudden movement on the stretcher interrupted the reprimand. The men looked at one another and lowered it quickly to the ground. Then the dead son began to speak.

FACING DEATH—WHAT YOU NEED TO KNOW

Death is an event every person will experience until Christ returns again. Death is the great equalizer, the most democratic of all experiences. We can fight it. We can avoid it for a time. We can argue, plead and bargain with it, but death is the one universal enemy. Death ultimately intrudes into our well-planned lives and changes things around, absolutely.

The death of her son must have raised many questions for the woman at Nain. *He was so young. I'm supposed to die before my son!* Heartbroken she must have asked, *Why me? Why this? Why now?* This woman came face to face with some realities of life—some that are so painful that we'd rather not talk about them, and some so good that we can't stop talking about them.

Loss is inevitable. In the middle of a cold December night, I received a phone call. As a pastor, a phone call in the night is never good. Good news can wait till morning; bad news necessitates waking others from their sleep. Expecting to hear about someone in my church, I was caught off-guard by the voice on the other end of the line. He introduced himself as the pastor of my parents' church. "Rick, your father has had a heart attack."

"Is he okay?" I questioned.

"Rick," he paused, "he has passed away."

A pastor is trained to deal with death and loss. Yet no matter the length of the training, no one, including trained professionals, ever feels fully equipped to deal with death, especially when it comes calling on someone you love. On that December night, I had to face the truth that no one can escape loss.

In college, a professor would often say, "Life is a series of losses and gains." He was right. But the longer I live the more I realize that there are a lot more losses than gains. And whatever their form, they are difficult to handle. When my father died I hurt. I was angry. I cried.

I know a little about how the widow of Nain felt with the death of her son. Loss creates a barren present. You are there, but something is missing. You are suspended between the past and the future, and try as you might, you can't grasp either.

Pain is intense. If you have ever broken your arm or separated a shoulder or sprained an ankle, you know what physical pain is all about. Pain is our body signaling that something is wrong. Physical pain often pales in comparison to emotional pain. The hurt associated with an abused childhood, a divorce, an abortion, a failed business, a miscarriage or a child dying often leaves one feeling the harshest and most severe pain.

Many counselors and psychologists agree that those who experience the death of a child experience the worst kind of emotional pain. I can't begin to fathom the severity of such hurt.

Joseph Bayly can. He lost three children: three weeks, four years and eighteen years old. In his book *The Last Thing We Talk About*, he mourned: "Of all deaths, that of a child is most unnatural and hardest to bear. In Carl Jung's words, it is 'a period placed before the end of a sentence,' sometimes when the sentence has hardly begun. We expect the old to die. The separation is always difficult, but it comes as no surprise. But the child, the youth? Life lies ahead with its beauty, its wonder, its potential. Death is a cruel thief when it strikes the young."

And when that thief comes, those left holding the empty future, like the widow of Nain, feel the sadness and the hurt and want to lash out at someone or something. Elisabeth Kübler-Ross, author of *On Death and Dying*, remarked that all hospital chapels should be converted into "screaming rooms." Losing a loved one frequently fills us with anger. We begin to ask theological questions. Where is God? Doesn't he understand? Doesn't he care? Pain plays havoc with our spirituality. When we encounter intense pain our sense of God's presence is usually the first thing to get out of focus and the last thing to come back into focus.

Can't you just hear the widow of Nain walking down the road wondering, *God, why is this happening? Why did you take my young son? What am I going to do now? How am I going to survive?* We want to blame someone for our pain. Sometimes we accuse God of being the source.

Jesus feels our pain. When we accuse God of our pain, he can take it. He knows our hurt and he suffers with us. He can deal with any offense, even death.

The one thing that stands out so visibly to me in this encounter Jesus had with the widow is that he "saw her" (Luke 7:13). This woman never called for help, did not exercise faith and sought no miracle. Yet Jesus saw her sadness, her grief and her hurt. He did not look beyond her, like we have a tendency to do. He really saw her.

Why is it that we interpret the presence of death as the absence of God? Why do we think that if the body is not healed, then God is not near? Somehow we have developed this warped theology that God delights when his children suffer. I've had many people come to me and ask, "Where was God when my son (or daughter) died?" I say that he was at the same place when his son was murdered. God is close to the heart, carrying the wounded and hurting soul. Then I lovingly say that God knows their pain. I try to help them see that their pain has temporarily eclipsed the reality of God's presence. In time, as the pain subsides, they will be able to see the love and feel the embrace of a grace-filled God.

William Sloan Coffin, a pastor in the Boston area, stated it more eloquently at the funeral of his teenage son. He said:

Hemingway wrote, "The world breaks everyone, then some become strong at the broken places." My own heart is mending. . . . Some have come to me and said, "I just don't understand the will of God." I say to them, "Do you think it was the will of God that Alex never fixed that lousy windshield wiper of his, that he was probably going too fast in such a storm, and there are no streetlights on that stretch of road, that there is no guardrail separating the road and Boston Harbor?" The one thing that should never be said when someone dies is, "It is the will of God." Never do we know enough to say that. My own consolation lies in knowing that when the waves closed over the sinking car, God's heart was the first of all hearts to break.

Jesus not only saw the widow of Nain, "his heart went out to her" (Luke 7:13). He didn't just acknowledge that she was in pain, he suffered with her. A woman with sorrows met the man of sorrows. Jesus knew the lonely walk she would have to walk all alone. He knew because he had been down and would continue to walk that same road too. Let me remind you that Jesus has experienced all the pain we will ever experience. He knows what it is to cry out and to pray with loud sobs. He wrestled with feelings that nearly tore him to pieces. He has suffered loss, rejection and heartache.

God sees you and he feels for you. When you hurt, he hurts. When you are in pain, he is in pain. His love for us moves him to great compassion.

That day in Nain, Jesus crossed the path of a funeral procession. In so doing, he raised a mother's only son to life. But the miracle wasn't for the boy; it was for the mother. Jesus raised a dead man to life, not to bring attention to himself, but to show compassion toward this woman.

When Jesus Showed Up

Jesus came upon this woman in the crowd in a rather dramatic fashion. But Jesus does not always work in such seemingly dramatic ways. Sometimes the sense of the Savior comes gradually;

this has been the case in my life. The Savior often crosses the path of our lives gently and unexpectedly.

During such times I'm not really conscious of Jesus' presence. But as I look back on those dark and devastating moments, I begin to understand that the Savior is walking with me.

Even when we do not have words to express our hurt and can find no sentiments to pray, God comes to us in our grief. He holds the keys to life and death. It was he who spoke to the widow and to her dead son in Nain that afternoon. And it is the same voice that wants to speak to us.

9

A REAL GAME
OF HIDE-AND-SEEK

Jesus Overcomes Our Insecurities

*J*esus entered Jericho and was passing through. A man was there by the name of Zacchaeus; he was a chief tax collector and was wealthy. He wanted to see who Jesus was, but being a short man he could not, because of the crowd. So he ran ahead and climbed a sycamore fig tree to see him, since Jesus was coming that way.

When Jesus reached the spot, he looked up and said to him,

"Zacchaeus, come down immediately. I must stay at your house today." So he came down at once and welcomed him gladly.

All the people saw this and began to mutter, "He has gone to be the guest of a 'sinner.'"

But Zacchaeus stood up and said to the Lord, "Look, Lord! Here and now I give half of my possessions to the poor, and if I have cheated anybody out of anything, I will pay back four times the amount."

Jesus said to him, "Today salvation has come to this house, because this man, too, is a son of Abraham. For the Son of Man came to seek and to save what was lost."

LUKE 19:1-10

One Sunday I preached a message on how Christians need to stop playing hide-and-seek, how they need to be vulnerable with one another. It was a well-crafted sermon with stirring stories and convicting applications. I was feeling pretty good about my performance until I got home that afternoon and my wife confronted me with stinging accusations: "You don't practice what you preach! You are not open with others and me. You are always guarded, only revealing what you want people to know. In reality you are tighter than a steel drum."

I had been caught and I knew it.

Ministers live in a world of tension. We have to balance our message with our behavior, and sometimes the two don't match.

Granted we can cover up our weaknesses and failures with many of our church members. But seldom can we fool our spouse or our children. They are up front and center stage watching our lives—seeing the discrepancies and shortcomings. Jesus is sitting next to them.

AN UNPRECEDENTED VISIT

A chill filled the morning air of Jericho—the cosmopolitan city stood tall only a few miles from the ruins of the ancient city where the walls came tumbling down when Joshua fought his battle. The bazaars were opening. Merchants were sweeping out their stores. Traders were quick about their business. Farmers were bringing their dates, myrrh and balsam into the city for export to the East.

Rich and fertile plains surrounded Jericho. It was a wealthy city, "the fattest in Palestine" according to first century historian Josephus. It was a commercial hub for people and wares going to Jerusalem and all points beyond. Everything and everyone had to go through Jericho. It represented one of the most important taxation centers in all of Palestine.

Selling was on the minds of many of Jericho's residents, but *seeking* was on the mind of Jesus as he made his way through the village. Jesus "came to seek and to save what was lost" (Luke 19:10).

The crowds swelled as Jesus walked down the main street. Jostling for position, they wanted to see him, to touch him, to hear him.

But one man who had the same desire could not get close enough. He was Zacchaeus, a tax collector and a Jew.

Rome occupied Israel, and Rome was primarily interested in

how much money they could wring out of the country. But instead of having Romans collect taxes, they would enlist indigenous people to perform the job. Zacchaeus, like most tax collectors, had become greedy and dishonest. His great wealth had come by economically raping his own people. He was hated and despised, a traitor. He had heard about Jesus befriending sinners and tax collectors. Word had spread that a tax collector in Galilee, Levi (a.k.a. Matthew), had joined the band of Jesus.

Zacchaeus was also vertically challenged, a short man. Wanting to see Jesus, Zacchaeus's height kept him from seeing above the crowd. His stature, however, had not kept him from climbing to the top of his world. Perhaps he wanted to compensate for his size, so he clawed his way to the top of his profession's ladder—he was the chief of the tax collectors. He had stepped on anyone who stood in his way. Zacchaeus was not a sweet little man; he was a formidable character with relentless drive to get his way.

Now, king of the hill, he had wealth and power, but he had no friends. All he knew was loneliness and sadness.

He wanted to catch a glimpse of Jesus. How could he? Up ahead at the bend in the road was a sycamore tree. So with a boyish eagerness he shinnied up the tree. Because the branches of the tree were strong and wide-spreading, and because it produced many lateral branches, it was an easy tree for Zacchaeus to climb, and he could easily be hidden. Knowing and being known was his greatest fear and, interestingly enough, his greatest longing.

Jesus was coming his way. Calmness exuded from his demeanor. He laughed easily. His eyes sparkled. He didn't look like a king, and yet there was something regal about him.

Zacchaeus could hear him clearly as he came closer. He could see the white of his eyes. He could reach down and touch him. Then Jesus stopped and looked up. At first, Zacchaeus drew back, trying to hide. But there was something compelling about this man, something that drew Zacchaeus out, something that communicated that he would be safe with the Savior. Coming out of hiding, Zacchaeus saw the love and compassion in Jesus' eyes.

"Zacchaeus, come down immediately," Jesus requested (Luke 19:5).

Oh, he's going to get it now, onlookers thought.

Zacchaeus climbed down the tree. The crowd parted as he made his way toward Jesus. Zacchaeus felt the darkness of his soul and the emptiness of his heart. For years he had rendered unto Caesar; now he must render unto Christ an account of himself. And he knew that his account wasn't very good. The ledger was filled with extortion, cheating, skimming. His life was about money. And the bottom line was a bankrupt life.

But Jesus was not there to do an audit. He was looking for something else. He was seeking a soul that had been crushed, a heart that had been bruised, a life that had been trampled.

"I must stay at your house today," Jesus continued (Luke 19:5).

"What did he say?" one man asked another. "Did he say he wanted to visit the tax collector's home? Is he going to eat with a sinner? I can't believe it."

Jesus and Zacchaeus walked down the Jericho road together. Zacchaeus welcomed Jesus into his home. The walls Zacchaeus had erected all came down. In one moment he was exposed to the sin of his past and granted freedom for the future. His heart of greed was filled with the grace of God. He then went out on another limb: "Look, Lord! Here and now I give half of my possessions to the poor, and if I have cheated anybody out of anything, I will pay back four times the amount" (Luke 19:8). What had taken a lifetime to accumulate was liquidated in one sentence of devotion. When Jesus looked him full in the face, something passed between them that changed his life. All the old hurts and indignities faded into nothingness. All the achievements, the prominence, the great house and the financial security passed into meaninglessness. Only the presence of the Savior mattered.

Centuries earlier the walls of Jericho came tumbling down at the shout of Joshua's trumpets. On this day the wall of a rich man's heart came tumbling down, too.

ARE YOU UP IN THE TREE?

Imagine that instead of Zacchaeus, it is you up in the tree. You long to see Jesus, and yet part of you is afraid to see him, because you know your life doesn't quite measure up. You are half-hoping Jesus will see you and half-hoping he won't. If Jesus were to come your way today and see you hiding, what would he question you about?

Are you hiding? The old adage is true: Our walk must match our talk. This is what my wife pointed out to me after my sermon on vulnerability. My actions did not match my words. To be honest, I have caught myself in other lies. I exhort others to have a daily quiet time, but some weeks I struggle to find the time. I challenge others to share their faith in a personal way, but I can go stretches of time without talking to one single person about their relationship with God. My congregation respects my teaching, but if they knew the whole story what would they think? Sometimes I hide behind a clean suit, a warm smile and a marked-up Bible.

We all hide—from parents and police, from bosses and

spouses, from teachers and coaches. And sometimes, maybe even most of the time, we hide from God. We want to cover up our flaws and fears. We want to run and hide like Adam did when God showed up in the Garden of Eden. We are prone to hiding. And then we wonder why we feel so abandoned and alone.

This was Zacchaeus. He had been hiding all these years, just as he was hiding in the Sycamore tree. He was trying to cover up his insecurities, his fears and the painful rejection from his past. He hid behind his ambition, wealth and power. He was quite good at hiding. So are we.

Are you lonely? Zacchaeus had amassed quite a fortune. But his wealth could not purchase the kind of meaningful relationships for which he longed. In his ambition he cut himself off from one of the most important things in life: friendship. He had drawn his circle closer and closer until only he was left. He felt the pain of loneliness. On top of the world, he was all by himself.

We are no different. We cry out for friendship and companionship. We have affluence but we don't have meaningful relationships. We have enough activities to occupy our calendars and enough gadgets to fill our time, but we lack those friendships that make life bearable.

Are you hurting? Aside from obvious problems such as blindness or lameness, Zacchaeus was the only person in the entire

New Testament noted for having a physical handicap. When Luke, the doctor, informs us that Zacchaeus was a short man, he must have been *extremely* short for his size. He quite possibly could have been a midget or a dwarf to receive such notice.

Put yourself in his shoes. People can be thoughtlessly cruel about disabilities, can't they? Zacchaeus must have been the butt of many jokes. He was probably chosen last for games and laughed at by the prettiest girls. Was it these hurts that drove him? Was he overcompensating for his stature?

Many a financier has been driven to achieve in the business world because her parents or teachers told her she would never amount to anything. Many a high-ranking military officer has attained recognition because he was a failure on the playing field or the dance floor. Many leading politicians got where they are today because of thwarted hopes or ambitions somewhere along life's way.

We, too, like to be noticed, approved, embraced; and, if this doesn't happen naturally, we work harder to make it happen. If we could peel back the layers of ourselves, my guess is that we would expose the motivating force as painful hurt of the past.

JESUS CHANGES OUR BEHAVIOR

Can you imagine the buzz around Jericho after Jesus went to

Zacchaeus's house? Can't you just hear the vendors, the merchants, the other tax collectors saying, "Did you hear what happened to wee little Zacchaeus? He gave away his fortune. He gave money to all the people he extorted. He even sent some money down to the poor house!"

We don't know what happened in Zacchaeus's house that day. Presumably Zacchaeus had his staff prepare a meal. Perhaps he and Jesus had a pleasant conversation on the veranda looking out over the lush groves of date trees.

All the writer tells us is that at the end of their time together, Zacchaeus announced his plan to give half of his possessions to the poor and fourfold to the defrauded. What an incredible change of behavior. The grasping, selfish, devious and conniving Zacchaeus became the generous, giving, sharing Zacchaeus. His generosity did not result *in* salvation, but rather was a result *of* salvation.

How did it happen? It happened because Jesus came to seek and to save what was lost. And what happened to Zacchaeus can happen to us when Jesus crosses our paths.

Jesus has come to find us. Jesus, like a shepherd who can't stop searching for one lamb even though he has ninety-nine in the fold, is looking for us. We may keep on hiding, but he can't seem to stop seeking.

The story of Jesus and the human race is one of hide-and-seek, only we get confused sometimes about who is IT. A bumper sticker proclaiming "I FOUND IT" was popular years ago. In a strict theological sense, the slogan is backwards. The truth is, IT found ME. By all outward appearances, Zacchaeus was seeking Jesus, when all along it was the other way around.

When Jesus finds us we are changed. When we come out of hiding we can be fully known, and when we are fully known we can be tenderly loved, and when we are tenderly loved we are completely changed.

We can get the courage to stop hiding when we understand the depth of Jesus' love. That is what happened to Zacchaeus that day in Jericho. He saw the love of Jesus and that love got him out of the tree and on his way to becoming a new person.

A part of being found is admitting that we struggle and fall. Some of the most positive remarks I receive from people following a message are when I admit that I have made mistakes. Granted I don't hang all my dirty laundry out each Sunday, but when I do share appropriately about my struggles, I acknowledge that I am a fellow struggler, and many can readily identify with me. It is a freeing experience. I, too, begin to understand the depth of Jesus' love.

Jesus has come to befriend us. Zacchaeus wasn't the kind of person you invited to Sunday dinner. When he walked down the street, people looked the other way; mothers moved their children out of his path; men looked down with contempt, murmuring his name and spitting into the street as he passed by. The religious people just shook their heads and thanked God they weren't like "that awful man Zacchaeus."

What a shock, then, when the rabbi Jesus crossed the path of this depraved and deplorable man Zacchaeus and invited himself over for brunch. A pious man was going home with the biggest sinner in town. Unheard of! Unthinkable!

Jesus had a way of defying conventions by befriending people that society has tossed in the trash: a profane fisherman like Peter, a revolutionary like Simon the Zealot, and now a corrupt tax collector like Zacchaeus. All felt the embrace of friendship from Jesus.

Notice Jesus' approach. We might expect him to say, "Zacchaeus, if you'll clean up your life, change professions, and pay back what you owe, I'll come to your house. I won't come now; it would look like I'm condoning what you've done. Frankly, I can't afford the criticism it would cause, so clean up your life and then I'll come over."

But Jesus does not make this demand. The Savior insists on befriending Zacchaeus even before Zacchaeus gets respectable.

Jesus came to free us. All those years, Zacchaeus was under the power of sin, most specifically the sin of materialism. He was trapped. He had been led to believe that money would make him happy. He had been hiding in the pursuit of wealth, perhaps out of a legitimate desire for significance and security. But it had so controlled his life that it caused him to hurt others and himself. When he is found by Jesus and knows the friendship of the Savior, he's finally set free from the power of money in his life.

In his great novel *The Robe*, Lloyd Douglas used the story of Zacchaeus to describe the liberating impact that Jesus makes on us. Zacchaeus promised to give away all his money. What did Jesus say to him? Douglas wrote: "Nobody knows. . . . Maybe he didn't say anything at all. Perhaps he looked Zacchaeus squarely in the eyes until the man saw—reflected there—the image of the person he was meant to be." That's exactly what salvation does for us: it sets us free to be the people God originally intended us to be.

Jesus came to accept us. All these years Zacchaeus had been hurting. He had endured the brunt of people's jokes, the harshness of their stares. He had been pushed around and beaten up. He had been stepped on so often that now he was determined to step on everyone who stood in his path.

He longed for someone to accept him in spite of his deformity, to respect him as a person. We are no different, are we?

There is no pain so great as the pain of not being accepted. A ten-year-old wrote Dear Abby about the pain of life on the playground: "All my life I have been chosen last. That's my problem. . . . Why don't they just hang a sign on me that says, 'Reject. Last one to pick gets me.'" But when a reject is chosen by someone, a life gets changed.

SEEING JESUS FACE TO FACE

When Zacchaeus crossed the path of Jesus that day in Jericho, something connected between these two men. In the warm and loving embrace of Jesus, pain and hurt melted away. His successes and accomplishments meant nothing. Only the presence of the Savior mattered.

Can you imagine what an encounter like that would do for us? We wouldn't look in the mirror wishing we were someone else. We wouldn't scheme to get ahead so people would think we're really somebody. We wouldn't build so many walls to protect our fragile selves from others. We would feel connected with the Savior. We would celebrate life and ourselves and God, all at the same time.

Francis McNutt, in his book *Healing*, writes about a young woman whose worries about her appearance had nearly caused a mental breakdown. She could no longer look in a mirror without thinking she was ugly and that other people were rejecting her because of that. Her failed relationship with her father badly affected her self-image. She didn't feel like a lovable, worthwhile human being.

McNutt taught her how to pray for Christ's healing in her life, and she practiced this kind of praying for several days. Finally she had to speak to her father. Sitting in front of him she cried. She told him her struggles. Her father put his arms around her—the first time she could recall his having done this—and the tears rolled down their faces for several minutes as they stood clinging to each other. Afterward she and her father were able to communicate as never before. She went back to work with a new hope and resplendent courage. Each day as she looked in the mirror she felt better about herself. Her whole life blossomed from having been cured in the depths of her heart.

Zacchaeus's story was like this one. His whole life changed as a result of meeting Jesus. He walked away from that encounter a new man, a different man. He didn't need props anymore. He gave away his fortune. He didn't need to live in a big house. He made restitution with those he had cheated and abused. He didn't need to show off or look down on anyone. He was a changed man.

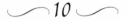

~ *10* ~

WHAT IF IT ISN'T TRUE?

Jesus Removes Our Doubt

*N*ow Thomas (called Didymus), one of the Twelve, was not with the disciples when Jesus came. So the other disciples told him, "We have seen the Lord!"

But he said to them, "Unless I see the nail marks in his hands and put my finger where the nails were, and put my hand into his side, I will not believe it."

A week later his disciples were in the house again, and Thomas was with them. Though the doors were locked, Jesus came and stood among them and said, "Peace be with you!" Then he said to Thomas, "Put your finger here; see my hands. Reach out your hand and put it into my side. Stop doubting and believe."

Thomas said to him, "My Lord and my God!"

Then Jesus told him, "Because you have seen me, you have believed; blessed are those who have not seen and yet have believed."

Jesus did many other miraculous signs in the presence of his disciples, which are not recorded in this book. But these are written that you may believe that Jesus is the Christ, the Son of God, and that by believing you may have life in his name.

JOHN 20:24-31

$\mathcal{W}$hat if Christianity isn't true?" asked the speaker at the chapel service when I was a student at Samford University. I, like the speaker, was reared in a Christian home. I, like him, was in the ministry. I, like him, knew that faith in God was what got me to heaven. My parents had faith, my church extolled me to have faith, my professors encouraged me to greater faith. I even preached in churches most every Sunday proclaiming a faith and persuading others to accept it. *But what if it isn't true?*

I suppose the nonbeliever must wrestle with the opposite question, "What if it is true?" What if there is a God one is to believe in, to hope in? What if there is a heaven and a hell? What if what separates the inhabitants of each is a matter of belief?

I struggled with the speaker's haunting question, "What if it isn't true?"

I guess I knew in my head that it was true, but I wanted my heart to be convinced as well. I was supposed to hear God's voice in the Bible and to talk with him in prayer. But I heard nothing. My prayers felt like an aborted flight that never reached its destination. I wanted more. I wanted more than someone else's experience. I wanted to experience God for myself. I wanted him to become real.

That night, after hearing the chapel speaker, I pondered his question. I visited a favorite spot of mine atop a mountain that looked back across the valley toward the university. It was dark. The air was warm. The stars were flickering. I paced back and forth asking God to show himself to me. I did not want to work up a feeling. I wanted to experience the real thing. I wanted to know once and for all if the Christian faith were true. I wanted God to break in on me.

He did not. I did not hear any voice. I saw no omen in the sky. Finally, I went back to my dorm room and crawled into bed. I continued to wrestle with the question, "What if it isn't true?" I continued to study, pray and preach most Sundays in small churches, proclaiming a faith in God. All the while, I did not stop hoping that God would show up and reveal himself to me.

What I experienced that night and the days that followed is not much different than what Thomas, one of Jesus' disciples, sought. Doubting Thomas and I share several similarities. We both have doubts and questions, and we're both skeptical. Thomas wanted Jesus to show up and prove himself real just as

I want God to break through my heritage and traditions to prove that the Christian faith is true. He wanted a firsthand experience. I also wanted a firsthand experience, and who doesn't?

THE STORY OF DOUBT CONFRONTING REALITY

Petrified with fear, ten disciples were huddled together in the upper room. The door was securely locked because the ones who killed Jesus might come after them next. Their nerves were on edge.

So much had happened on this day. Mary Magdalene had gone to the tomb of Jesus and found the stone rolled away. She told Peter, so he and John had raced to check out the grave for themselves. The stone was rolled back just as Mary had said. Peter and John went home confused and dazed, unable to make any sense of what they had seen. Mary stayed a while longer in the garden, to contemplate, to meditate, to reflect on what it could mean. *Why? Why would they do such a cruel thing to a lovely man?* Suddenly she bumped into a man she thought was the gardener. But it was Jesus, and off she went. "I have seen the Lord!" she proclaimed (Matthew 20:18).

Had she seen the Lord? Was her love making her hallucinate? Who could know? The disciples were unsure. They had seen him crucified. They watched the burial. How could he be alive? Gathered in that room behind locked doors, they were plotting their next move when suddenly Jesus stood in their midst. They were startled. Was it a ghost? It looked like Jesus, but he was dead. Their hearts were pounding.

Jesus spoke to them, "Peace be with you!" (John 20:19). *Shalom*—the most common greeting in Palestine—put the fearful band of followers at ease. Then he did the most outlandish and unexpected thing: "he showed them his hands" (John 20:20). He did not keep them guessing for even one minute. He showed them his side, where a Roman spear had dug into the flesh below his heart.

The disciples saw that he was alive, all except Thomas. He was not present at the upper room meeting with Jesus on resurrection day.

Where was Thomas? Was he off somewhere grieving, needing to be alone? Was he visiting the sick and imprisoned, clothing the naked and feeding the hungry? Was he wandering around in anger knowing his hope had died with Jesus? Maybe he got the time of the meeting wrong or misplaced the directions. Maybe he was chronically late.

The other disciples caught up with Thomas: "We saw him, Thomas, really, we saw him. He's alive. We touched his hands and felt his side. Thomas, it's real. He is the Savior!"

Thomas wouldn't buy it. *Impossible! How could a man crucified on a cross, buried in a tomb, rise to life? Things like that don't happen. It can't be true.* Thomas boldly asserted to his friends, "Unless I see the nail marks in his hands and put my finger where the nails were, and put my hand into his side, I will not believe it" (John 20:25).

Thomas raised tough questions, the kind that made everyone around him nervous because no one knew the answers. Thomas refused to silence the integrity of his mind. He was a realist. His world left no room for the resurrection. He had seen Jesus die and he would not settle for any hearsay comments or secondhand faith. He was a skeptic. "Unless I see . . . I will not believe." He had to have a firsthand experience. He knew that if he were going to invest more faith in Jesus, he would have to have his own encounter.

One week later Thomas got the time and the directions right. Same room. Same group. Same locked door. Same appearance. Jesus stood before them again. A collective gasp was heard in the room. And again Jesus uttered, "Peace." Everyone relaxed—except Thomas. The other men had been through this experience before, but not Thomas. It was new for him. He was scared stiff. Jesus looked at Thomas. Wide-eyed wonderment filled the soul of Thomas. *Could it be true? Is it really him?* Then Jesus walked to Thomas. Reaching out and taking Thomas by the hand and then placing it in his hands and on his side, Jesus spoke. There was no tone of anger or ill will. Jesus' compassionate voice spoke precisely to Thomas's doubt. Jesus said, "Put your finger here; see my hands. Reach out your hand and put it into my side. Stop doubting and believe" (John 20:27).

Jesus did not send a well-written tract on belief. He did not order belief. He did not offer a theological argument. Jesus simply showed up. He met Thomas's honest doubt with real evidence. He offered Thomas what Thomas really needed—a real encounter, a real experience.

Tears of joy rolled down Thomas's face, as he looked upon the wounds of Jesus. And all he could do was fall to his knees in worship, confessing that Jesus was truly his Lord and God. It was perhaps the greatest affirmation of Christian faith ever uttered. "My Lord" would have been a sufficient title for Jesus. But Thomas spoke to Jesus as Israel had spoken to Yahweh—"My Lord and my God" (John 20:28). It was a pivotal moment for Thomas. These are the words of a doubter turned believer, a cynic turned worshiper, a truth searcher confronted by Truth incarnate.

THOMAS COULD BE OUR TWIN

What an injustice history has done this honest man. Call him frightened Thomas, or confused Thomas, or questioning Thomas, or seeking Thomas. John tells us that his nickname was "the Twin." If he is anyone's twin, he is yours and mine. We should have no difficulty identifying with his struggle.

Jesus acknowledged Thomas's doubting when he said, "Stop doubting and believe" (John 20:27). But doubt is not to be feared; in fact, doubt is to be welcomed. Doubt is part of faith's process. Someone has said, "Doubt is the mother of faith." Doubt is our faith grasping for truth and honest answers. Doubt is the scuffle between faith and life. Left untended doubt can become destructive, but addressed honestly and sincerely, doubt is beneficial in our faith walk.

Thomas is not alone with his questions and skepticism. In fact, all the great people of the Bible doubted at one time or another. The prophets doubted. Job doubted. Most of the psalms are about David's questioning and wondering when God will show up in his life. Jesus doubted. In the garden the night before his execution, Jesus questioned God's plan. All ten of the disciples in the upper room doubted Jesus. Why would they not believe Mary? Why would they have the upper room door locked? They only difference between them and Thomas was that Thomas verbalized his doubt.

Clearly, it is as much a part of the biblical tradition to ask *Why?* as it is to affirm our faith. In fact, our faith is only strengthened as we question and honestly search for answers and God himself. Some people, like Thomas, feel more comfortable with question marks than exclamation marks. We will search and come to the point where our faith combines both questions and exclamations. It is that search that leads us to God.

Silencing honest uncertainty can be a destructive step. Repressed doubts have a high rate of resurrection. Doubts that are plowed under the soil of our souls tend to grow new roots and come to the surface again and again until they are treated.

Although Jesus strongly warned against unbelief, he never condemned Thomas for his doubt. Jesus knows that doubt and belief are sometimes compatible. Thomas's story reveals that faith matures because of, not in spite of, doubt. For in asking the questions of life, the richness and depth of the answer is revealed.

Thomas, in the end, thanked God for his doubt. It propelled him from an infantile faith to a mature faith—a faith of his own, not passed down from others. While Thomas could not see the end of his life's journey and surely doubted again from time to time, he walked away from his experience with Jesus taking one faith step at a time. His faith came alive as a result of the vibrant experience of seeing Jesus alive.

SOURCES OF DOUBT

Doubt can assault our faith from a variety of sources. The different breeds of doubt have the same goal in mind—to destroy our faith. But each needs to be unearthed before we learn how to deal with the doubts.

Emotional doubt springs from pain. Expressed in the phrase "I'm hurting," our emotions (vivid imagination, changing moods, erratic feelings, intense reactions) rise up and cloud the understanding of faith. Triggered by hardship and suffering, doubt forces us to look at our world. How can we make faith fit with the painful realities of life? Someone we love dies. Children face hunger. We are crippled by disease. We lose our job or a marriage. We cry out, "Where is God? And why doesn't he help?"

Experiential doubt springs from insecurity. Experiential doubt is expressed in the phrase "What difference does it make to me?" We doubt whether we matter, whether things can be changed, whether hard work and sacrifice really pay off. When we have lost the conviction that our lives are important, we have lost the conviction that what we believe matters. Thomas lost Jesus and lost his reason for living. Obviously a simple straightening out of a doctrine or two won't solve this kind of plight.

Volitional doubt springs from self-willfulness. This kind of doubt is related to the inability to make certain choices. It is often expressed by saying, "I'm resisting." It is revealed in an attitude of appreciation for the facts while not being willing to make the appropriate decision indicated by them. Doubt springing from unbelief may sound oddly redundant, but doubt and unbelief are not necessarily the same. Sometimes our doubt is faith staggering for firm footing. Sometimes, though, doubt is mutiny against faith. In the first case, we are like the man who said to Jesus, "I do believe; help me overcome my unbelief!" (Mark 9:24). In the second, we are like unbelieving Israel of whom it was said, "The message they heard was of no value to them, because those who heard did not combine it with faith" (Hebrews 4:2). Volitional doubt, then, grows out of willful disbelief.

Thomas said, "I will not believe," rather than "I cannot believe." Doubt is one thing; it is an honest questioning. God has never turned away the questions of a sincere searcher. Unbelief digs its heels in the presence of evidence and refuses to accept it. It turns its back on examination and refuses to ask questions. Unbelief can close the door on God working in one's life.

Intellectual doubt springs from lack of evidence. Intellectual doubt, expressed by the phrase "I'm thinking," concerns itself with the evidence for Christianity and issues related to the truthfulness of the faith. For Thomas, while he believed in the teachings of Jesus, he doubted the bodily resurrection of Jesus. That event went beyond his rational thinking. But after seeing the facts—the resurrected Jesus standing before him—Thomas stopped doubting once and for all and believed.

Moral doubt springs from disobedience. Whether consciously or subconsciously, we sometimes use doubt to rationalize disobedience. At those times we say, "I won't believe." When we face the demands of Scripture, we are not quite sure of our faith. We express this doubt through intellectual questions when, in fact, it is simply disobedience. We cover our sinfulness with a coat of doubt.

MAKING SENSE OF DOUBT

While we should not put doubt on a pedestal, it can be used in a positive way and lead to some exciting times in our spiritual adventure. Used properly, doubt can assist us in finding the truth and discovering that God is real. If we have an honest heart and an open mind, God will meet us at our point of need.

Many believers affirm the faith of their fathers and mothers.

I did. Having grown up in a Christian home, reared by godly parents and encouraged by a loving church, I became a believer.

A reporter once asked a famous theologian: "Sir, you have written many huge volumes about God. How do you know it is all true?" The learned scholar responded, "My mother told me." I know what he meant.

The smooth road of my Christian walk hit some potholes in college when my faith was challenged. It came to a climax that day in chapel when the speaker asked, "What if Christianity isn't true?" Was my faith genuine, or was it the secondhand faith of my parents? After seeking God atop the mountain that night, I visited with a godly professor the next day. I explained my dilemma and my questions. He encouraged me to read the Gospels and ask the question, "God, if you are real, please show yourself to me." I began to read and over time God revealed himself. In time my faith became stronger and fuller and more rewarding. It moved from a secondhand religion to a firsthand experience. I walked beyond knowing about God to knowing Jesus personally. He became real. My faith became genuine.

As I look back on my period of questioning and doubting, I realize that it was a worthwhile process. Doubt took that which had been given to me (my faith from my parents), tested it in the fire ("God, if you are real, show yourself to me"), and gave it back to me as mine, tempered, strong and able to stand the assaults of the world (genuine, authentic, firsthand experience). Doubt brought me an authentic faith.

Thomas developed a faith that transcended his doubts. He went on to proclaim his faith, according to legend, as an evangelist to India.

What was done for Thomas, and for me, can be done for you. If you are honestly seeking and sincerely searching, God will meet you in your doubts. Don't look for signs in the sky or voices in the night. God has a way of showing up when you least expect it. And when he does, he doesn't say, "Just believe me." He says, "Look at my hands and my feet." His presence will transform your doubt into a vibrant faith.

CONCLUSION

Will you have the faith to believe that Jesus will cross your path?

Unbelief has a way of making us miss the obvious. Remember the story of the Battle of Waterloo? Allied troops under General Wellington fought Napoleon on June 18, 1815, at the Battle of Waterloo, a village in Belgium just south of Brussels. News was transmitted by the use of lights across the English Channel to anxious Brits awaiting the outcome. The words were spelled out, "Wellington defeated . . ." Then a fog, typical of England, fell over the channel. England thought the battle was lost and the dreadful news was spread quickly, throwing the land into despair. But when the fog lifted they could see the final word, "Wellington defeated Napoleon." And the mood in Great Britain changed from one of tragedy to triumph. The whole country exploded in thunderous celebration as the news was relayed. Napoleon had been defeated.

Unbelief is like the fog that fell on the English Channel. The fog prevented the truth to come through gloriously and triumphantly. The fog of unbelief can prevent us from seeing Jesus crossing our paths. Imagine winning a victory and not even knowing it.

We think that Jesus will not cross our paths. It's just too good to be true. We do not lack evidence; we lack hope.

Will you look for Jesus? Will you see what he can do in us— renew our depressed spirits, restore our hurting hearts, cleanse the hurt from our past, forgive all our grievances, give life to a dead existence—meet us at our point of greatest need?

Do you see the Savior? He's showing up in your life, crossing your path, meeting you when you need him most.